Madhavi Menon is professor of English at Ashoka University, and writes on desire and queer theory. She is the author of *Infinite Variety: A History of Desire in India*; *Wanton Words: Rhetoric and Sexuality in English Renaissance Drama*; *Unhistorical Shakespeare: Queer Theory in Shakespearean Literature and Film*; and *Indifference to Difference: On Queer Universalism*. She is also the editor of *Shakesqueer: A Queer Companion to the Complete Works of Shakespeare*.

THE LAW OF DESIRE

RULINGS ON SEX AND SEXUALITY IN INDIA

MADHAVI MENON

SPEAKING TIGER

SPEAKING TIGER BOOKS LLP
125A, Ground Floor, Shahpur Jat, near Asiad Village,
New Delhi 110049

First published by Speaking Tiger in 2021

ISBN: 978-93-5447-115-5
eISBN: 978-93-5447-123-0

10 9 8 7 6 5 4 3 2 1

Typeset in Garamond Premier Pro by SÜRYA, New Delhi
Printed at ...

For Papa, the progenitor of law,
and Achan, the embodiment of love

Sculptures at Khajuraho, Madhya Pradesh.

Love does not ask about caste or religion, love is the enemy of the law.

—Bulle Shah (circa 1720)

The fact that there is a body of sex laws which are apart from the laws protecting persons is evidence of their distinct function, namely that of protecting custom.

—Alfred Kinsey,
Sexual Behavior in the Human Male (1948)

Citizens of a democracy cannot be compelled to have their lives pushed into obscurity by an oppressive colonial legislation.

—*Navtej Johar vs Union of India* (2018),
striking down the criminality of consensual acts
'against the order of nature' in Section 377
of the Indian Penal Code

Roster

Preamble

Can a woman choose whom to marry if her father disapproves of the match? Does sex remain sex when it becomes work? Can a man become a woman because he feels like one? Is it the law's task to ensure heterosexuality? Does reproduction need to be regulated? These are some of the many questions with which the law is faced, and upon which it pronounces. Ranging from deliberations over Bills to the passage of Acts, from hearings in the lower courts to appeals in the Supreme Court, from cases under British rule to those post Independence, the law has been deeply entangled with desire. But how, and with what assumptions, are legal pronouncements on desire made? How does the law appear when looked at from the vantage point of desire? What are the consequences of specific laws on the texture of desire?

The recent judgment in *Mobashar Jawed Akbar vs Priya Ramani* (2021) makes clear the multiple assumptions about desire that go into a legal verdict. In February 2021, Justice Pandey cleared a journalist on charges of defamation for publishing an account of sexual harassment. By ruling that women can and should speak publicly about incidents of sexual harassment, the Court sent a clear signal that we must not tolerate unwanted sexual attention. In noting that public posts can legally be classified as being for the public good, the Court made the question of sexual harassment a question of the public domain itself. And by arguing that social status does not provide behavioural impunity, the Court recognized that sexual predators can lurk behind even seemingly respectable facades. All this is to the good.

But despite its social concern, the judgment is also sexually dubious. Or more precisely, its attitude to desire is cause for some concern. Justice Pandey's judgment is a response, he says, to the sexual shame that women feel when they are subjected to harassment. In order to counter 'The Shame', the learned judge suggests a turn to the epics of the *Mahabharata* and *Ramayana* to uncover historical instances of 'respect for women'. It is startling that the judgment adduces 'respect for women' as one of the themes of the *Ramayana*, even though Sita is shunned in the text for being the bearer of 'The Shame'. This is also the text in which Sita is made to go through a trial by fire in order to prove her sexual virtue. And it is also the text in which, despite passing the trial by fire, Sita is shunned because her demonstrated virtue cannot quell the paranoid fantasies of the citizenry around her.

Undeterred by these facts, the judge goes on. As an example of 'respect for women' he cites the *Valmiki Ramayana*'s account of Laxman being asked to describe what Sita looks like. Laxman responds to the question by saying he does not know what she looks like because he has never looked at her beyond her feet. The judgment holds this up as an example of respect for women. But what this tale from the *Ramayana* suggests is a phobia about sex that disproportionately attaches to the bodies of women. Laxman does not look beyond Sita's feet because she is married to his brother, and is therefore sexually owned by another man. He draws a circle around Sita to keep her desires within patriarchal control, and warns her not to step outside its ambit. When she does, Sita is punished for transgressing against male control. In other words, the tale of Sita from the *Ramayana* is a glaring example of a moral regime in which women's desires cannot be trusted because they lead to disaster for men. Women must be protected from their desires in order for men to preserve the status quo. This sexual morality polices desire without preventing its abuse, and signals an official recognition of women as men's property. As we see in the *Akbar vs Ramani* case, even a celebrated judgment on sexual harassment operates within this dubious terrain of sexual conservatism. And it also dabbles in religious majoritarianism by harking back to the *Ramayana*, especially in a case involving a Muslim man.

Picking 'desire' as the term with which to represent these many facets of sexuality, politics and culture might seem like an odd choice, particularly since the law itself rarely uses the word. But 'desire' is also the term that can most fully evoke these multiple affective and historical registers without being reducible to any one of them. Desire conjures up sexual acts and orientations while also not being synonymous with them. It points to embodied genders and enacted sexualities while also including social aspirations and legal standards. Desire can straddle the body, mind, social structures and cultures at large. Desire suggests pleasure while also encompassing pain. Like its subject matter, 'desire' is immense. Which is why we have so many laws to deal with it.

But these laws do not simply thwart desire—they also enable it. Law promises official recognition if desire can be reduced from multiplicity to a specific category of identity. For instance, law confers rights based on specified gender and sexual orientations—you are rewarded for being heterosexual and for marrying within your caste, religion, and community. If you do not abide by the constraints of hetero-sex, binary gender, and caste and religious endogamy, then you are punished with administrative burdens; even when law allows people to define their desires as non-binary and non-heterosexual, it upholds a social norm that makes it difficult for people to act on those desires. Homosexuality, for instance, is no longer criminalized in India. But it has to act within the normatively legal structure of privacy in order to assure itself of State protection. Being legally recognized also means being legally policed.

Another way in which the law enables desire is more perverse, and therefore, more fascinating. By putting obstacles in the way of desire, law ensures its flourishing multiplication. Think of all our most famous love-stories: Heer-Ranjha, Layla-Majnun, Romeo-Juliet. They all have in common lovers in opposition to an unfriendly law; indeed, in Nizami's twelfth-century Persian rendition of *Layla-Majnun*, the poet notes that Majnun 'was a lover, and love knows no laws'. Desire in these stories increases not only despite the obstacles put in their way by family and social pressure, but also *because* of them. The law inadvertently encourages the militant, unruly, and threatening aspects of desire to emerge in full force—literature and history are full of such examples.

This is why law wants desire to be categorized because desire poses the biggest threat to the rule of law. By sneaking past social constraints of caste and religion and gender and orientation, desire threatens to unravel the social fabric itself. Law wants to maintain the status quo, while desire can overturn hierarchies. The law protects social structure, while desire threatens to undo it. Even the simplest possible question posed from the vantage point of desire has the ability to upset social categorization. For instance, the progressive *NALSA* legislation in 2018 on the category of the 'third gender' in India confers civic rights on third gender people. But the law cannot bring itself to ask why gender should be tied to civic rights that are due to any citizen of the country. Why does the law need to know if I am a man or a woman or neither or both in order for me to get a ration card? What is the relation between my gender and how much subsidized rice I can buy? This is precisely the line of thought the law disallows because it questions fundamental categorical assumptions.

But there is hope yet. Despite the law's delight in definition, it is riddled with caveats and exceptions. It is not enforceable in any uniform manner, and petitions can result in drastically different judgments. The law is thus less rigid than it pretends to be because its fundamental activity is that of 'interpretation'. Equally, desire is often more acquiescent than we might like it to be. Under pressure, it disavows multiplicity in order to inhabit straitjacketed categories sanctioned by the State. Desire can thus appear to be legally dutiful despite its unruliness, while the law can in fact be more chaotic than the rigidity of its demeanour.

Such are the paradoxes of law and desire that this book will explore. Law defines the social, while desire threatens to disrupt it; the law of desire is, therefore, both a necessity and an impossibility. The sheer volume of laws on desire suggests that the more law tries to control desire, the more it fails to do so. Or rather, the more that law attempts to differentiate between justified and unjustified desires, the more it gets caught up in the swirls of its own subject. If we add to desire's stable of terms the unstable immensities of society, religion, and culture in which desire is embedded, then we get some sense of the task in which the law of desire is immersed. Desire spreads across multiple laws and diverse subjects. It finds its way into the cracks of commercial and criminal and civil law, depending on whether we consider desire to be property, a fundamental trait of our personality, or a right guaranteed by the Constitution. Indeed, one reason for the ever-expanding scope of the law of desire is law's inability to *locate* desire. On the one hand, desire is assumed to be a private affair that is internal to the individual. But on the other hand, it is legislated upon as a public matter. Private desire is hopelessly entangled with public expectations. The private becomes legible only when it is public.

These public adjudications have taken shape around four adjectives that define the law's relation to desire: Criminal, Immoral, Obscene, and Unnatural. All these are terms that laws and legal judgments have used while addressing desire. The very idea that there should be criminal laws to deal with desire underscores the nexus between criminality and sexuality. The charge of immorality follows hot upon these criminal heels when desire runs counter to social expectations. Obscenity is then set up as an umbrella term within which to trap all manner of physical and intellectual deviance; it is a moving target because obscenity is never fully defined by the law. And the shifting grounds of nature make all desire potentially unnatural. Based on these four adjectives, bodies come to be endowed with truth or falsity, desires are approved or disapproved, sexualities are accepted or criminalized.

What emerges from these four adjectives, and from the conundrums and paradoxes, private and public, pleasurable and punishable, that they generate, is that even as the laws of desire number in the thousands, there can be no single and final Law of Desire. Instead, we have multiple attitudes to desire that inform legal thought, and diverse assumptions about gender, society, culture, and desire that underpin both laws and judgments. This book is an attempt to lay bare some of those attitudes and assumptions.

Criminal

On December 21, 2016, a twenty-four-year-old woman walked into a courtroom in Ernakulam with her newly-wedded husband, and the two-judge bench of the Kerala High Court reacted with anger. Recording his response, one of the judges termed the marriage 'a totally unexpected event' that was designed to fool and mislead the Court. He pointed to discrepancies in the marriage certificate, insisted that the details should be verified, and noted his 'dissatisfaction at the manner in which the entire exercise was accomplished'. The judge claimed that the defendant had not said a word about her impending marriage, even though she had been in court on December 19, the very day of her wedding. And despite being active on Facebook, the bridegroom had not publicly posted any photos or updates about the wedding. Building on his 'dissatisfaction', the judge ordered a police inquiry into the background details of the bridegroom, and also declared the marriage to be null and void.

To try and understand why the High Court reacted in this manner, let us go back a few months. Early in 2016, a writ of habeas corpus had demanded that the Kerala High Court track down and bring K.M. Asokan's daughter, Akhila, back to her parental home. Akhila appeared in court on her own steam as the defendant in *Asokan K.M. vs The Superintendent of Police*, but she appeared as Hadiya, and refused to go back home. She had converted to Islam, which her parents would not allow her to practice at home. The case dragged on for a few months, even though it should have been dismissed as soon as Hadiya appeared. After all, a writ of habeas corpus demands that the court produce the person whose existence is in question; as such, the Court should have declared the case to be closed as soon as Hadiya appeared before it. Instead, the judges tried to adjudicate where and with whom Hadiya should live, and how and by when she should complete her course in homeopathic medicine. The case dragged on for several months.

And then something changed: Hadiya married a Muslim man named Shafin Jahan, with whom she attended the court hearing on December 21, 2016. The Kerala High Court was aghast at this development and went into a tizzy of activity. But why did the young woman's marriage rattle the learned judges so much?

When the case first began, Hadiya was not married. The Kerala High Court seemed a bit sad about her conversion to Islam, but it was also inclined to let it stand: 'The question of faith and religion are matters of personal conviction and this court does not consider it necessary to interfere in such matters that are personal to Ms. Akhila.' Even as the Court insisted on referring to Hadiya as Akhila, and could not resist making snide remarks about how it is unusual for a young woman to be so interested in matters of religion, it considered religion to be a 'personal' affair in which the Court should not interfere.

But after Hadiya's marriage, the personal case became very public. The Court could not believe that Hadiya's choice of religion had extended also to an expression of marital desire. Nor could it believe that she had got married without the 'permission' of her parents. Indeed, the Court reminded us that even though Hadiya is twenty-four years old, we must not forget that 'a female in her twenties is at a vulnerable age. As per Indian tradition, the custody of an unmarried daughter is with the parents, until she is properly married'. Also, according to the learned judges, marriage is the 'most important decision' in a woman's life, and must only be finalized 'with the active involvement of her parents'. A grown woman is weak and in need of her father's protection until she gets *properly* married to a man who will then take over the mantle of protector. But when the father is Hindu and the husband is Muslim, the mantle, it seems, cannot be passed on properly. Suddenly, all notions of what a woman can and cannot choose to do are furiously qualified. Her 'personal' choice is no longer valid when it comes to an expression of sexual desire. Even more, her sexual desire gets subjected to the scrutiny of the police, and Hadiya's 'private' marriage becomes the criminal jurisdiction of the State itself.

Indeed, what was earlier described as her privacy now gets converted into 'secrecy'. The marriage seems to have been conducted in a hurry, the judges say. They insist that 'the entire episode is shrouded in suspicion'. The burden of proof is placed on the defendant's shoulders: 'Unless the suspicion is cleared the detenue cannot be permitted

Hadiya and Shafin Jahan, 2018. Photo is reproduced with permission of the photographer; image published on *Scroll.in* on March 13, 2018 (See https://scroll.in/article/871772/we-want-to-show-society-our-marriage-wasnt-a-farce-hadiya-shafin-jahan-say-after-being-reunited).

to go with the person who is seen to be accompanying her now.' Just as Akhila cannot be called Hadiya, Shafin Jahan cannot be called her husband. He is demoted from occupying that intimate role to being 'the person who is seen to be accompanying her now'. Hadiya's private marriage is declared null and void, and first the police, and then the National Investigation Agency, are publicly ordered to probe the entire affair.

Despite its shocking assertions about the weakness and vulnerability of women, despite the patriarchal cast of its comments, and despite its unconscionable verdict annulling the marriage, the Kerala High Court performed one very useful function in its judgment. It asserted publicly that desire is not private.

The appeal against the Kerala High Court judgment finally reached the Supreme Court in 2018, where a three-judge bench struck down the earlier verdict. Interestingly, the Supreme Court's decision too was based on the notion of privacy, but from a different perspective. Quoting his own judgment in the *Justice K.S. Puttaswamy vs Union of India* case of 2017—popularly known as the privacy judgment—Justice D.Y. Chandrachud reiterated that the freedom to take decisions about 'family, marriage, procreation and sexual orientation are all integral to the dignity of the individual', and should not be interfered with. Denouncing the Kerala High Court verdict, Justice Chandrachud noted firmly that 'the High Court, in the present case, has treaded on an area which must be out of bounds for a constitutional court. The views of the High Court have encroached into a private space reserved for women and men in which neither law nor the judges can intrude'. Marriage is a private matter between individuals, asserted the Supreme Court judgment. However, it simultaneously allowed the ongoing NIA investigation into Shafin Jahan's antecedents. Desire is private, it seems, until it runs counter to the prevailing social norms. Then it becomes, not only very public, but also criminal. Hadiya is 'free' to marry Shafin, but now that she has, the Supreme Court will investigate the validity of that desire.

Hadiya's story moves back and forth between these two poles of private and public. Legally, she is free to choose what religion to follow and who to marry after the age of eighteen. But the Kerala High Court's discomfort with her 'private' choices also shows us how public such decisions really are. Both religion and sexuality are simultaneously understood to be private and public. And in India, their combination has been endowed with a particularly explosive character since the time of the British. In its most recent avatar, the spectre of 'love jihad' has been raised in relation to every cohabitation of desire and religion; indeed the governments of four states—Uttarakhand, Uttar Pradesh, Himachal Pradesh, and Madhya Pradesh—have passed ordinances that stipulate as much as ten-year jail sentences (for men) in cases of 'inter-faith marriages with the sole intention of changing a girl's religion'.[1] Four more states—Karnataka, Assam, Haryana, and Gujarat—have promised similar laws. The canard goes that Muslim men are wooing 'unsuspecting' Hindu women and making them convert to Islam on the pretext of love. This was the bogey raised in relation to Hadiya as well—both that she is a vulnerable and susceptible woman, and that terrorist organizations are out to recruit people like her. Indeed, the phrase 'love jihad' occurs in almost every news story about the Hadiya case.

What is interesting, though, is that Hadiya's story follows the opposite trajectory of an alleged case of 'love jihad'. Instead of falling in love and then converting, Hadiya first converted to Islam and *then* found Shafin Jahan on a matrimonial website. To put the emphasis a little differently, *Hadiya* converted to Islam and then found herself a husband online. Her case thus defied two basic rules of good behaviour for women: she showed that she has a mind of her own, and that she can act on her desires. She decides which religion to follow and which person to marry. The all-male bench of the Kerala High Court was angered by these extremely public and intensely private decisions made unapologetically by a woman. It therefore went ahead and criminalized them.

While the Indian Constitution technically protects religious freedom, in reality, the State polices the process of religious conversions. (In India, the Intelligence Bureau keeps track of them.) And nowhere does this policing kick in more viciously than when it comes to marriage. The introduction of religion marks marriage as a domain in which an allegedly private desire is placed firmly in the public sphere: mixing desire and religion opens both up to legal scrutiny. Even when the law tries to help desire overcome religious boundaries, it ends up reinforcing those boundaries. For instance, the Indian government passed the Special Marriage Act in 1954 because people were finding it difficult to marry across caste and religious divides (they still cannot marry within the same gender). The Act, brought into effect purely because private desire is a very public affair, allows couples to marry for love rather than according to their parents' will. This is a noble sentiment, and has been of use to thousands of couples across the country—it allows them to step outside the fetters of religion and caste.[2] But the law cannot officially condone the screwing up of religious and caste boundaries. So even as it provides a back alley in which parents can be sidestepped, the requirements for marrying under the SMA continue to be far more stringent than for marrying under personal laws. Legally, the normative expectation is that the majority of marriages in India will and should take place in accordance with religious sanction and parental blessing.

This expectation that family knows best spills over into a series of related aspects of the law. It even partly explains the current push to 'reform' surrogacy laws in India. Despite suggesting reformation, the Surrogacy (Regulation) Bill that was passed by the Lok Sabha in 2019, approved by the Union Cabinet as the Surrogacy (Regulation) Bill, 2020, and now awaiting ratification in Parliament in 2021, seeks a complete ban on commercial surrogacy. Its provisions in 2019—since amended slightly—will allow only a 'close relative' to carry a surrogate child to term, and that too only once in her lifetime. Needless to say, this 'close relative' would not be paid for her labour (the revised Bill allows couples seeking surrogacy to cast their net a little more widely than just close relatives, but no matter who acts as the surrogate, payment, other than for medical needs, is prohibited). Further, both the people wanting the child and the woman providing the child have to be part of a (heterosexual) married couple (again, the revised Bill allows widows and divorcees too to seek surrogate babies, but only if they have previously been a part of a lawfully-married couple). Why all partners involved in surrogacy need to be or have been married, and why they ideally should be closely related, one does not quite know. But the Surrogacy (Regulation) Bill makes it clear that in matters of marriage and reproduction, the heteronormative family knows best. This is why LGBTQ couples, single people, and those in live-in relationships will be forbidden from engaging a surrogate's services under the new law. Instead, married women will have to shoulder the burden of unpaid 'ethical surrogacy' for the relief of their male brethren.

A legal system that makes women bow down to men was what Hadiya's father was banking on. But he was also banking on precedents set by laws in India to criminalize Muslim men's desires. The ease with which the Kerala High Court and the Supreme Court—despite arriving at opposite judgments—could support an NIA investigation into Shafin Jahan, indicates how deeply entrenched this conviction of criminality is in our legal system.

In fact, no desire is legally more criminalized in India today than desire by and for Muslims. There have been, over the years, several non-state actors who have taken it upon themselves to police this desire. Some of these vigilantes even visit the courts that perform weddings under the Special Marriage Act in order to look at the notices of intended marriage, and then inform the family of the girl if she is a Hindu marrying a Muslim. But the latest in the spate of state-sponsored criminalization of Muslim desire is the Muslim Women (Protection of Rights on Marriage) Act of 2019. Like so many laws in which the use of the word 'protection' actually means its opposite, the 'Triple Talaq' Act, as it is colloquially called, makes illegal talaq-e-biddat, in which a man can divorce his wife by saying the word 'talaq' three times.

The practice of triple talaq is outlawed in most Muslim countries, and is barely in use in India. There are no reliable sources for the number of cases of triple talaq here, and almost all available sources suggest the number is small. Still, the government felt the need to introduce a Bill outlawing this largely-dormant practice. Let us agree that it is indeed good to outlaw triple talaq since it inordinately privileges the husband's desire over the wife's.[3] But why *criminalize* the act of triple talaq instead of just outlawing it?[4]

Is it because criminalizing Muslim men's desire is the *goal* of the Act rather than an unintended side-effect? 'Whoever pronounces talaq...upon his wife shall be punished with imprisonment for a term which may extend to three years and fine,' says the new law. It does not seem to be enough to say that triple talaq will no longer be legal tender in India, and that women 'divorced' in this manner will not be considered divorced at all. The point of the law is to state unequivocally that Muslim men (who resort to triple talaq) are criminals. Even more, the rhetoric deployed by the Muslim Women (Protection of Rights on Marriage) Act is that of the downtrodden Muslim woman suffering at the hands of the criminal Muslim man. And so the self-declared ambit of the Act is to 'prevent the continued harassment being meted out to the hapless married Muslim women due to talaq-e-biddat'. Its message is clear: Muslim men are criminals and Muslim women are in need of protection (from them).

This fantasy of 'saving' women also animates the High Court's judgment in the Hadiya case. Not only do the judges repeatedly ignore the fact that Hadiya is a grown woman, but they also insist that she has to be saved, both from herself and from the clutches of a shady Muslim 'terrorist' organization run, we presume, by allegedly criminal Muslim men. But let us leave Hadiya alone for a while after her wedding, and stay with the question of divorce.

The triple talaq bill presents itself as saving hapless Muslim women from criminal Muslim men. Its rhetoric suggests that Muslim women have always been deprived and Muslim men have always been depraved. In this context, it is interesting to remember historian Rohit De's observation that the 'construction of Muslim personal law as backward is ironic, given that Hindu conservatives, in the 1950s, had attacked the "progressive" Hindu Code Bill on the grounds that the draft code was "90 per cent Muhammadan law". In the 1950s, divorce, inheritance by women and guardianship rights of the mother—while radical innovations to Anglo-Hindu law—were established precepts of Anglo-Mohammadan law'. In fact, he describes the Dissolution of Muslim Marriages Act of 1939—an Act still in effect in India, Pakistan, and Bangladesh—as a 'radical piece of social legislation...[that] gave Muslim women the right to sue for divorce...almost two decades before Hindu women, and [in which they] could sue under a larger number of grounds than those available to their Christian counterparts in India and women in Britain'.

In other words, Muslim law was recognized by many Hindus as being progressive, perhaps even overly so.

In 1929, ten years before the passage of the Dissolution of Muslim Marriages Act, the All India Women's Conference and the All India Muslim Ladies Conference (Anjuman-e-Khawateen-e-Islam) called for laws to reinforce Muslim women's rights of inheritance and divorce. While almost all Muslim members of the Central Legislative Assembly supported the Bill, De points out that 'Babu Baijnath Bajoria, the representative for Indian Commerce, expressed his horror at a law [the DMMA] that made divorce so much easier'. Bajoria feared that if the law were to be passed (which it was), then Hindu women too would clamour for equal rights to divorce (which they did not). The ease with which Muslim women's rights were secured owed largely to two factors. First, under Quranic law, Muslim women have more rights than their counterparts professing other religions. For instance, even after marriage, husband and wife among Muslims are legally separate persons with separate estates and legacies, and they can enter into separate contracts. Muslim marriage is itself a contract rather than a sacrament, and as such, it is already a legalized exchange rather than a sacralized bond. Muslim weddings require two witnesses and the consent of the bride and groom. No religious figure is involved in the proceedings, hence the famous aphorism, *miyan-biwi raazi, toh kya karega qazi* (if the husband and wife are willing, then what role does the religious man play)?

The legal situation on the ground, then, has been

weighted substantially towards Muslim women, who have enjoyed rights unheard of by their Christian and Hindu peers. In fact, when the Hindu Code Bills in the 1950s sought to secure inheritance for daughters, the primary criticism was that such a radical practice amounted to an Islamization of Hindu law.[5] Similar yet completely opposite objections were raised against the proposal to banish polygamy among Hindu men. If monogamy must be required of Hindus, the claim went, then it must be required of Muslim men as well. Polygamy flourished legally among Hindu men until the passage of the Hindu Marriage Act in 1955; in fact in 1961, 5.7 per cent of Muslims apparently practised polygamy, while the figure among Hindu men was higher at 5.8 per cent. Other than the relation of envy that Muslim men might continue to 'enjoy' what Hindu men were about to lose, there were also several other reasons cited against banning polygamy. Among them, as Archana Parashar points out, was the argument that according to the shastras, Hindu men need sons in order to facilitate their passage into the next world after death, and thus men without sons must be allowed to marry over and over again until they have a son. Other reasons offered were protection of the Hindu faith—it was thought that polygamy was so attractive that Hindu men would convert to Islam in order to hold on to their wives. Or, in a more feminist vein, that the men would remain Hindus while the wives would be reduced by law to the status of concubines. Economic necessity—multiple wives are needed to perform the business of farming in villages—was also another defence against legislating against Hindu polygamy.

But how have we even come to talk about laws in relation to 'Hindus' and 'Muslims'? When did we start passing laws in relation to religious communities rather than, say, geographical entities or secular citizens? And why do we do it?

It has often been pointed out that if Hindus and Muslims did not exist, then the British would have invented them. Abhinav Chandrachud notes that in 'the census in Gujarat in 1911, some 2,00,000 people described themselves as "Mohammedan Hindus"'. He adds that 'several Muslims in India...considered themselves governed not by the Shariat in personal law matters, but by their own customs which were analogous to Hindu personal law'. The present-day political divide between Hindus and Muslims ignores the fact that these categories were created by and for the convenience of our colonial overlords. The British fashioned Hindus and Muslims as 'always' having been cohesive categories hermetically sealed-off from one another. Several different sects got lumped together under the administrative umbrella of 'Hindu', and several factions got melded together under the aegis of 'Muslim'. This consolidation and classification began with India's first British de facto Governor-General, Warren Hastings, who in 1772 declared that 'Mahomedans' and 'Gentoos' (his version of 'Hindus') would be governed by their own laws. But what were these laws and how to determine them?

Hastings set in motion a process in which the Brahminical texts—principally the shastras and the *Manusmriti*—were understood to be the laws of the Hindus, while the Quran and shariat were considered the law of the Muslims. This textualization of the law had several effects. First, it often disregarded the more malleable customs on the ground that might have been at variance with what texts said; in other words, it ignored how people lived, and it made rigid what had been much more fluid (in relation to Muslim women's rights, however, textual law was actually more permissive than customary practice). Second, it privileged high-class texts to which most people had no lived relationship; the law was thus overly Brahminical. And third, it created the *legal* categories of Hindus and Muslims where such clear-cut divisions had not existed before.

Prior to the British, laws were applied to both territories and peoples. The Mughals, for instance, had a variable structure of laws throughout their territories that were adapted by local customs that criss-crossed religions. The British tried to ensure a smooth transition from Mughal laws to their own, but the smoothness was in name only, and completely ignored the pluralistic practices followed by the Mughal courts. In Rohit De's argument, even though the British claimed to be continuing 'to apply the law of Hindus and Muslims to matters of inheritance, marriage and religious institutions...the analogy was false, since the Company state itself administered the law of each religious group'. In other words, even as the British governed by using

'Muslim law' and 'Hindu law', both sets of laws were identified and defined by the British themselves.

To prove that only British law—based, they said, on reason rather than religion—was good enough to frame general laws with which to govern the realm, the British undertook a two-pronged strategy. First, they painted Indic religions as irrational and primitive. And therefore, second, they limited the reach of such religions to the realm of 'personal' laws (which they publicly mandated). Where Indians had tended to live in and out of multiple legal systems across all realms of life, they were now divided into 'Hindus' and 'Muslims', and told to live strictly according to 'their' laws as interpreted for them by the British. According to Julia Stephens, 'the [1864] Indian Law Commission for the first time explicitly specified that Hindu and Muslim laws would be limited to "succession, inheritance, marriage, and caste, and all religious usages and institutions." It domesticated religious laws, by associating them primarily with the family. And it communalized these laws by limiting their applicability to a narrow group of co-believers'. 'Personal laws' became the legal equivalent of what are anatomically termed the 'private parts' of the body: avowedly central but effectively kept out of sight.

Fostering such religious division encouraged open hostility between Hindus and Muslims, and ensured India's docile submission to the British. In order to secure British rule, Indian social and religious pluralism was reduced to a legal binary, and almost overnight, India got separate personal Hindu and Muslim laws.

Religion and desire became fused, even as religions and their desires got separated. A hundred and fifty two years later, when the Kerala High Court stated its displeasure at the fact that Hadiya 'had got married according to Islamic religious rites...[even though her] parents are Hindus', they were speaking this language of separate personal laws and legally separated desires.

The Kerala High Court judgment also traded in another bogey that currently has the country in its grip: the spectre of terrorism. Indeed, one of the judgment's pet themes was the father's 'concern' that Hadiya might be 'smuggled' out of the country to Syria and made to join the Islamic State. Hadiya's father alleged in his second writ petition 'the involvement of radical Muslim organizations that are engaged in transporting girls who are converted to Islam, out of India'. When he had stated this as a concern in his earlier petition, the Court downplayed the possibility of such an occurrence by saying that Hadiya did not even have a passport. But now, the Court portentously observed, the 'question that crops up...is whether the marriage that has been allegedly performed is not a device to transport her out of this country'. Once again, we are at a point of collision between an allegedly private marriage and a criminalizing nation-state. Religion and desire become flashpoints between communities and countries.

We have been here before.

In 1949, following upon the horrific and violent partition of India in 1947, and high-level discussions between the two countries, India and Pakistan passed an Ordinance to recover abducted persons on both sides of the bleeding border. In India, this Ordinance was converted into The Abducted Persons (Recovery and Restoration) Act. Even though the Act defined an abducted person as 'a male child under the age of sixteen years or a female of whatever age who is, or immediately before the 1st day of March, 1947, was, a Muslim', in

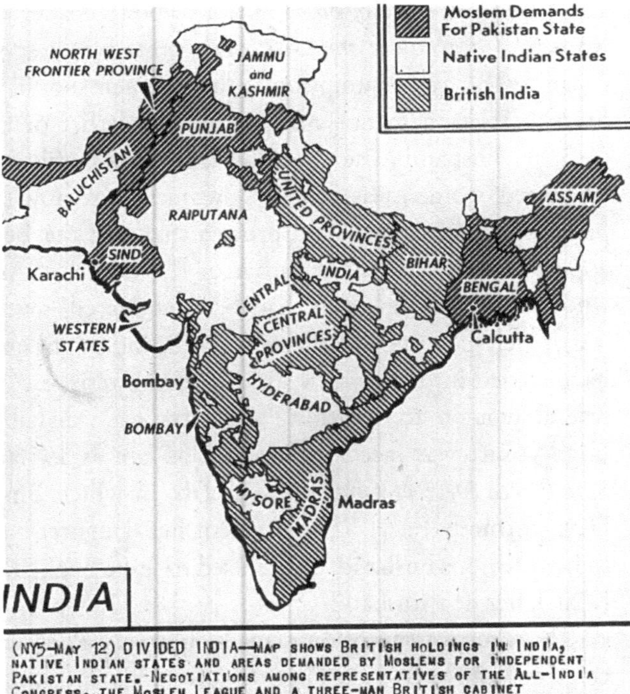

Source: Wikimedia Commons.

reality, the government's Central Recovery Operation was focused on women living with men of a different religion, all of whom were presumed to be 'abducted' women. These women so identified then needed to be 'recovered' and 'restored', often against their will.

In technical terms, these 'recoveries' were versions of the habeas corpus writ petitions filed by Hadiya's father since they all aimed at 'producing the body'. They were also based on certain presumptions about desire and women that connect the two legal events across seven decades. The first assumption is that women should be fixed in relation to one man, either the father or the (proper) husband. The shocking thing for families of 'abducted' women was that these women were now the property of other men in a process that had not been approved of by either the father or the husband. And while many women really had been abducted, several might well have gone of their own will, and might even have settled into their new unions, as the resistance of several women to returning suggests. The Allahabad High Court was faced with a case as late as 1953 in *Smt Bimla Devi vs Chaturvedi & Ors*, in which Bimla Devi (formerly Razia Khatoon) sent her daughter back to her previous husband, but refused to leave Bagh Shah Khatri, her new husband.

The second assumption made by both the Partition-era law and the Kerala High Court judgment is that women's desire cannot be trusted. Despite many women's unwillingness to return, both States inevitably insisted on putting them in camps and then returning them to their fathers or husbands because the women could not be relied upon to speak the truth. The women's insistence that they were happy with their new husbands, and often, new children, did not hold water with the authorities. All such statements were considered to be coerced and dismissed out of hand. Finally and urgently, women's desire was assumed to be a matter of national security. Retrieving abducted women was considered an issue of familial and national pride. Even when fathers and husbands rejected women for having become sexually 'polluted', even when women preferred their new union to their previous situation, and even when women refused to return, they were forced to because it was a matter of national pride that a country's women should be pure and in their proper place. In its role as protector and moral police, the State is coded as both masculine and heterosexual.

All these patriarchal assumptions about women, desire, and nationhood are underlined in the joint statement released by the prime ministers of India and Pakistan in 1947: '[We] wish to make it clear that forced conversions and marriages will not be recognised. Further, women and girls who have been abducted must be restored to their families, and every effort must be made by the Governments and their officers concerned to trace and recover such women and girls.' Women and girls are to be recovered from their current situations of unacceptable desire and restored to their families. The nation-state enacts laws to channel women's desires in lawful directions dictated by the legitimate family unit.

Conversion and marriage-after-conversion of *women and girls* are seen by all sides as being in need of legislation. Until the women and girls are restored to their proper men, the law will act as the man to protect them. In an almost exact echo—undermining and questioning women's desires—the Kerala High Court, seventy years later, asserts that 'this Court, *exercising Parens Patriae jurisdiction*, has a duty to ensure that young girls like the detenue are not exploited or transported out of the country' (my emphasis). The borders of women's desires and the nation alike are to be regulated by a masculinist State acting as a parent. Even as the Supreme Court criticized the High Court's use of parens patriae jurisdiction, it continued to act on the assumption that Hadiya's desires could be criminal in relation to the welfare of the nation. The more things change legally, the more they stay the same. For the law, desire is always potentially criminal.

IMMORAL

This is a Tale of Two Laws.

On a hot summer day in June 1948, Saride Narayana of Mukkamala village in East Godavari district got married. To celebrate his wedding, he commissioned a dance performance by a troupe of artistes consisting of eight dancers and six musicians. In 1950, a case against Narayana and the dancers reached the Madras High Court. The complaint alleged that the women dancers were devadasis—professional dancing women associated largely with religious sites of worship, whose existence had been outlawed. The judges tried the case under the Madras Devadasis (Prevention of Dedication) Act of 1947.

On another hot summer day a decade later, in May 1958, the Allahabad High Court was presented with a petition by Husna Bai against the newly-notified Suppression of Immoral Traffic Act of 1956 (SITA). This law prevented tawaifs—the north Indian secular equivalent of devadasis—from practising their trade. Tawaifs had for centuries been custodians of music and culture attached to the courts of Nawabs and Rajas in the north. This new legislation, Husna Bai claimed, would interfere with her right to practise the centuries-old profession to which she was heir.

From south to north, Madras to Allahabad, women were being prosecuted and threatened with prosecution under these laws, which were among the first to be passed by a newly-independent India. The Madras Devadasi Act, for instance, was passed four months after Independence, so clearly the legislators considered the issue to be of some urgency. But what exactly was the urgent issue that these laws were meant to address? What brought the Madrasi devadasi together with the Allahabadi tawaif and made them both subject to legal censure?

Perhaps we should begin with the acronym of the Act that Husna Bai was protesting in 1958: The Suppression of Immoral Traffic Act or SITA. In a neat linguistic move, SITA took as its name the aspirational ideal of Hindu femininity—Sita, the chaste wife of Rama. Despite her association with sexual purity, in the myth, Sita is discarded by Rama because she cannot prove beyond the shadow of a doubt that she is still pure after having been kidnapped by Ravana. Even though Sita goes through a trial by fire to demonstrate to her husband that her sexuality and his honour are both intact, the proof is deemed insufficient (this is 'The Shame' that was invoked by Justice Pandey in the *Akbar vs Ramani* judgment). Whenever Sita is upheld, then, as a marker of sexual morality, we remember that immorality too is attached to her. The law's recourse to the legend of Sita underscores that purity and immorality are never far away from one another. Like its namesake, SITA reinforces an obsession with the sexual purity of women. Written into the piety-drenched acronymic letters of the law itself is the belief in women's sexual immorality.

The Suppression of Immoral Traffic Act was

enacted early by the sovereign Indian state as part of its obligations to a United Nations convention. Titled the Convention for the Suppression of the Traffic in Persons and of the Exploitation of the Prostitution of Others, 1950, this treaty, as its name makes clear, equates trafficking in people with prostitution. Commercial sex is conflated with the forcible kidnapping and sale of human beings; as such, prostitution is criminalized even before it can be tried. This conflation between trafficking and prostitution has been the dominant narrative in the West. But even in India, the legal connection between trafficking and prostitution has become so deep-seated as to allow the interchangeable use of the two terms in legal judgments.[1] Thinking about prostitutes as trafficked women—despite empirical evidence to the contrary—invites indiscriminate governmental and non-governmental attempts at 'rescue and rehabilitation'. Indeed, the emphasis on 'rescue and rehabilitation' presumes, first, that prostitutes are victims in need of rescue. And second, that they would much rather be trained to perform some other kind of work. Commercial sexual activity was legislated against on the assumption that women would never *choose* to be prostitutes, so they must be victims in need of protection by the law. Neither the UN Convention nor SITA considered the possibility that commercial sex might be volitional rather than trafficked. Just as Sita's protestations are ignored and she is made to pay the price for patriarchal paranoia, so too do SITA and its descendants both disbelieve women and try to contain them within limited sexual boundaries.[2]

Nautch girl dancing with accompanying musicians,
Calcutta, India. Frank and Frances Carpenter Collection.
Source: Wikimedia Commons.

SITA was replaced in 1986 with the more neutrally-acronymized ITPA, or the Immoral Traffic Prevention Act, which also made 'prostitute' a gender-neutral term (though no man has yet been prosecuted as a prostitute in India under ITPA). All activities that support prostitution are criminalized in this Act, even though prostitution itself is not made illegal. If a woman wants to prostitute herself in private, then the law will not interfere. (Does this mean, then, that 'private trafficking' too is legally acceptable?) But if she does so in public—in a brothel or on the street—then the law comes down on that sex encounter with a force that is fierce. Police are authorized to shut down premises they think are being used for prostitution, and to arrest all those they suspect of living off the income of prostitution. The law is draconian to the extent that it snatches away the rug from under the feet of prostitutes, but it is reticent to the extent that it does not ban prostitution as such.

By not outlawing prostitution fully but making it impossible to practise it openly, the law suggests that prostitution in private does not upset the sexual applecart as much as prostitution in public does. When practised in private, prostitution suggests an individual moral depravity that can be explained away as one person's anomaly. This is not a sexual practice that can spread widely because it is restricted by space and constrained by the availability of resources. Non-sanctioned sex, or even sex for profit, does not agitate the law if it is practised by one woman in her own house. But when it comes to organized houses of prostitution, prostitution as a public business, prostitution as a visible and audible occupation, then the law shifts into gear. For the law, prostitution in public threatens to become a health pandemic.[3] Not necessarily in terms of physical disease, but in terms of moral rot.

And why might this be so? In legal fantasy, sex is synonymous with personhood: it forms the innermost and most sacred part of the self. The *NALSA* judgment in 2014 stated that 'we have to recognize the right of a human being to choose his sex/gender identity which is integral to his/her personality and is one of the most basic aspects of self-determination, dignity and freedom'. This belief is what gives rise to legal phrasings like 'outraging the modesty' of a person, and legal descriptions—purportedly in support of women—like the 'unethical and squalid business of prostitution'. It is also the reason why Justice Bachawat observed in 1966 that 'the essence of a woman's modesty is her sex. The modesty of an adult female is writ large on her body. Young or old, intelligent or imbecile, awake or sleeping, the woman possesses modesty capable of being outraged'. And as the judgment in *Pramod Bhagwan Nayak vs State of Gujarat* made clear in 2006: 'To recognise prostitution as a legitimate means of livelihood [will result in the] total destruction of a woman's personal identity, and her right to live as a free human being in a civilised society.'[4]

And so, when sex emerges from behind closed doors, suggesting that it can be public work rather than our most private and cherished attribute, it pokes holes in the law's assumptions. This is precisely because sex work—what the law calls immoral traffic—threatens to disrupt the legal language of morality. It stands at what Anne McClintock terms 'the flash points of marriage and market, taking sex into the streets and money into the bedroom. Flagrantly and publicly demanding money for sexual services that men expect for free, prostitutes insist on exhibiting their sex work as having economic value'. Sex work claims to be a profession, and as such, demands the respect accorded to other professions. In fact, Husna Bai's 1958 petition in the Allahabad High Court depended on the assumption that prostitution is work. If prostitution is a job, then, she claimed, SITA violates her fundamental right, guaranteed by the Constitution, to practise a profession.

For SITA, however, prostitution is hazardous to health: it threatens to make sex a public act rather than a private identity. If sex can be a profession, then far from making us who we *are*, it defines what we *do*. Prostitution is a job. As Rohit De points out, prostitution is routinely described by its practitioners with words that mean work: *kaam*, *dhanda*, *pesha*. Prostitution makes sex public. And that makes sex less the mark and measure of the private. This is perhaps the biggest challenge that prostitution poses to the law—it suggests that sex can be performed rather than felt. And far from expressing the authentic core of the self, sex might be an act to be sold to the highest bidder. This fear of sex as an act rather than an identity motivates laws like SITA and the Madras Devadasi Act alike. By announcing their mission as 'rescue and rehabilitation', laws against immoral trafficking seek to recuperate sex and contain it within a zone of residential and existential privacy. Anything else threatens the moral bedrock of society.

And this is the pivot: if sex no longer references a person's emotional core and does not translate into authentic intercourse, then there is no way for the law to control the *meaning* of sex. It could mean anything for anyone. It could mean different things for different women. Allowing sex to wander in public means its destination is no longer known. In response, the law forces sex back into the closet where its reach can be controlled. Saba Dewan points out that in Banaras, after SITA came into effect, several renowned and reputed tawaifs stopped performing altogether for fear of prosecution. Those who continued to perform could only do so in concealment: 'hastily bought thick curtains now covered the partially shut entrances to kothas that had, until recently, been open to all'. In order to escape censure, sex has to be moved out of the public sphere and back into a private space.

This move was directly challenged by Husna Bai's petition in the Allahabad High Court, which hinged on Sections 4 and 20 of SITA for placing unreasonable restrictions on her profession. Section 4 criminalizes anyone who is 'living with or [is] habitually in the company of a prostitute' and lives off the earnings of prostitution, including elderly family members, while Section 20 gives a magistrate sweeping powers to expel a prostitute from the area under his jurisdiction. Husna Bai—who openly declared herself to be a prostitute—claimed that Section 4 violates Article 15 of the Constitution, which prohibits discrimination on the basis of religion, race, caste, sex or place of birth, while the threat of expulsion under Section 20 goes against Article 19's guarantee of the freedom of residence. Despite agreeing with some of these arguments, Justice Sahai dismissed the case because Husna Bai had not yet been affected by the law. She had filed her case on May 1, 1958, the very day that SITA came into effect and before it had made any arrests.

In fact, prostitution in India has for centuries been

a public job rather than either a legally prohibited category of work or a morally sanctioned core of the self. Even more, as the *Kamasutra* makes clear, sex is something that one does rather than what one is. Veena Oldenburg highlights this notion of sex as work when she reminds us that the courtesans of Lucknow, classified by the British in the nineteenth century 'under the occupational category of "singing and dancing girls"... were [professionals] in the highest tax bracket, with the largest individual incomes of any in the city'. Added to this financial success is also sexual imposture; Oldenburg notes that during the course of their work, 'for many [tawaifs], heterosexuality itself [became] the ultimate nakhra and feigned passion an occupational hallmark'. For systems of thought that are invested in placing sex at the centre of our authentic selves, the idea of paid sex and feigned pleasure are terrible things to contemplate.

Against the current judicial notion of sex as being indicative of personal authenticity, scholars of Indian legal history like Prabha Kotiswaran take us back in time, to the rule of Chandragupta Maurya and the production of the influential treatise of statecraft, the *Arthashastra*. Compiled and set down between the second century BCE and the third century CE, the text describes ganikas as 'women who properly took to prostitution as an occupation... A Ganika was treated like a government servant [and] received a fixed government salary of 1000 panas per year'. Like their Lucknawi descendants many centuries later, the ganikas too were taxed on their income. In his *Kamasutra*, Vatsyayana devotes an entire book to outlining the lives and practices of courtesans as well as their training (which involved knowledge of the sixty-four arts outlined in the *Kamasutra*).

How did we get from the ancient *Kamasutra*'s professional courtesans to SITA's newly-immoral tawaifs? Kotiswaran notes that 'while in ancient India one witnessed the legalization of prostitution, during the colonial period, one saw the rise of the criminalization of prostitution'. In fact, she suggests that the 'British were amazed' by the high status accorded to prostitution in India. Bothered by so many of the sexual practices they encountered here, the British were aghast that prostitution was not considered immoral. In response, they legalized sexual prudery, criminalized prostitution, and attached moral judgment to sex without commitment.[5] According to Rohit De, the idea of the prostitute as a morally depraved person who insults her core modesty in order to make money, and who needs to be rescued lest her depravity spread like a disease, is entirely 'a creation of colonial law'. Sex as a set of continually-changing practices and frequently-honed skills was deemed by the British to be primitive. Instead, they insisted that all women must be 'protected' by being made to enter into the state of holy matrimony.

And they had help with their moralizing mission. Kotiswaran quotes a Dr W. Crooke—crook by name, crook by nature?—who points to a 'certain number of educated Indians, who have imbibed western ideas and education' and who, on the basis of their English education, separate themselves from the Indian heritage of prostitution. 'It is hardly an exaggeration', he says, 'that the great majority of India's inhabitants, representing orthodox and conservative opinion, still regard the profession, and those who follow it, with tolerance, and sometimes even with respect and approval.' This is why the project of building a modern nation had to move *against* the 'orthodox and conservative opinion' of a country that had historically respected prostitutes and their profession. Modern India had to be grafted onto a moralizing criminal law, one of whose first acts was to outlaw women's involvement in sex as a professional rather than emotional commitment.

The mode by which both SITA and the Madras Devadasi Act envisaged rescue and rehabilitation for prostitutes was, in a word, marriage. Section 2 of the 1947 Madras Devadasi Act states explicitly that prior custom notwithstanding, women who might once have been devadasis can now enter into legal marriages: 'Any custom or usage prevailing in any Hindu community... that a woman of that community who gives or takes part in any melam (nautch), dancing or music performance...is thereby regarded as having adopted a life of prostitution and becomes incapable of entering into a valid marriage [is] hereby declared unlawful and void.' The Act clears the way for all current and former devadasis to get married to human men as opposed to male gods. As Davesh Soneji notes, 'courtesans were... overwhelmed by the valorization of monogamy and domesticity in nationalist discourse', especially when conjugal domesticity was presented as the superior

A photograph of two devadasis taken in 1920s Madras. Reprinted with permission from PD-India (See https://en.wikipedia.org/wiki/File:Devadasi_1920s.JPG#filelinks).

alternative to their non-conjugal presence in the public sphere. Marriage and motherhood were presented legally as the only solutions to what the law regarded as unruly female sexuality. Even as late as 1997, a Supreme Court judge could say about prostitutes that 'marriage...[can] give them real status in society'.

This 'solution' of marriage ensured that sex could once again become *meaningful* rather than inauthentic. If a non-conjugal sexual space represents danger to the law, then the conjugal state is meant to restore sexuality to safety. This is perhaps why the most legally challenging category of sex workers are the married women who perform sex work on the side, often with the full knowledge of their husbands. Not only do they announce that sex is something they do, but also that there is nothing about marriage that precludes their having sex outside it. Far from being a haven against immorality, then, marriage is a bastion that has been, and can be, breached by sex work. Such a breach suggests that the traffic of immorality can travel in both directions, in and out of marriage. In short, marriage is not the monogamous haven that the law considers it to be. Indeed, one must read the law's reluctance to criminalize marital rape as the most stark instance of the law protecting the holiness of marriage despite much evidence to the contrary.[6] Might it not, in fact, be better to marry a god?

The term 'devadasi' translates literally as 'servant of God', and refers to women and girls who were dedicated to the service of a deity in a temple. The ire of the law has always been directed at the ceremony of 'pottukattu' that begins the dedication ceremony by tying the marital thread around the neck of the woman, thereby marrying her to the temple god. Whether or not this marriage has in fact taken place becomes central to determinations made under the Madras Devadasi Act. In 1950, when the eight women were taken to the Madras High Court along with Saride Narayana, the suit against them alleged that they were devadasis who were dancing in a temple. But the case was dismissed because the Court determined that the shoe did not fit on two counts. First, the pandal in which the dance took place could not be construed as a temple, the presence in it of framed images of gods notwithstanding. And second, the women said they had never been dedicated to an idol, so they could not be termed devadasis under the Act. They were never married to God, but would, we imagine, speedily be married to men, since that was the law's plan for their moral 'rehabilitation'.

In the historical record from the late sixteenth century onwards, devadasis were considered second only to the priests in the temple, and enjoyed financial independence on the basis of temple lands and revenues that were bestowed upon them. In turn, they often bestowed sexual favours on (mostly) Brahmin men associated with the temple. But 'devadasi' soon came to refer to any professional woman who sang and danced in public, whether or not she was associated with a temple. Not all dancing girls were dedicated to deities, and not all devadasis earned their money in temples alone—

they also performed in salons and at weddings. The war against 'devadasis', then, seems to be less exclusively against temple dancing, and more against non-conjugal sexuality, which became synonymous with public dancing. Indeed, Kunal M. Parker reminds us that the 'term "devadasi" was not employed commonly within Anglo-Indian legal discourse until the second half of the nineteenth century, and even then, it never dislodged the colonial label of "dancing girl"' that contemptuously described all professional artistes who happened to be women.

The cultural battle in relation to devadasis—broadly termed the 'anti-nautch movement'—started across the country in the nineteenth century, but only gained momentum in Madras with the introduction of Dr Muthulakshmi Reddy's 1927 resolution in the Legislative Assembly, which recommended that 'the Government undertake legislation to put a stop to the practice of dedication of young girls and young women to Hindu temples for immoral purposes'. This resolution became A Bill to Prevent the Dedication of Women to Hindu Temples in 1930, and then The Madras Devadasis (Prevention of Dedication) Act in 1947.[7]

Dr Muthulakshmi Reddy was the first woman medical graduate in the country, the daughter of a devadasi mother and a Brahmin father. She was also a staunch follower of Annie Besant and the Theosophical Society, from where she drew many of her ideas about the aspirational ideal of purity. Indeed, in her public speeches and letters, Reddy, like several other women abolitionists, insisted that the new nation requires pure women as citizens.[8] The crux on which 'purity' depended seems to have been marriage, which is why non-conjugal sexuality became the target of laws across the country. The modern nation was erected on the patriarchal grounds of what Soneji terms 'naturalized female chastity and marital fidelity'. Abolitionists were expected to lead by example, and thought nothing of trampling on centuries of aesthetic and social custom in their march to a post-colonial future whose terms had ironically been determined by the colonizers themselves.[9]

Highlighting the costs of this legal obsession with marriage, Kunal M. Parker notes that '[v]irtually all legal rights, duties, incapacities and disabilities in respect of [Hindu] women were constructed around marriage'. He adds that by 'constructing the "crime of dedicating girls to a life of temple-harlotry", Anglo-Indian courts exploited the polyvalence of the legal category of "prostitution" to the fullest extent. Temple dancing girls were represented as "prostitutes"—not as participants in a sex trade but in terms of Hindu legal norms according to which all female sexual activity outside marriage was designated "unchastity", "incontinence" or "prostitution"'. He suggests, daringly, that the creation of 'Hindu law' not only potentially designated all sex outside marriage as prostitution, but also all those whose sex lives did not revolve around marriage as not 'Hindu'.

Clearly, such a situation meant a loss of caste.[10] If sex is supposed to be authentic—an unshakeable truth about the self—then caste too is meant to be inviolably fixed, and each is meant to reflect the other. In fact, the primary text on which Anglo-Hindu law based itself—the *Manusmriti*—is obsessed with sexual preservation against loss of caste (for upper-caste men). Under the British, every caste was recognized as having legally protected practices. And so, whether or not 'dancing girls' should be recognized as having a caste became a matter of legal debate. If they were considered a separate caste (as some instances of Mitakshara law suggested they were), then their customs would have to be granted priority when they were at variance with textual law. Their matrilineal practices of ownership and inheritance would have to be respected. But the courts chose instead to place devadasis outside caste altogether. They emphasized female immorality in their legal dealings and defined devadasis as 'degraded Hindu women'. Temple dancers lost caste as prostitutes whose sexual activity was in direct opposition to marriage. Their properties were laid open to claims by men in their family who would otherwise not have inherited any of it.[11] The idea of sexual 'degradation' thus worked both to imprison the women and embolden the men, and explains the large number of inheritance cases that were tried under the Madras Devadasi Act in the twentieth century.

The Madras Devadasi Act laments that 'such practice [of devadasis], however ancient and pure in its origin, leads many of the women so dedicated to a life of prostitution'. This notion of an originary purity that has devolved over time into caste and sexual degradation is written into the law itself to justify its existence.

The language of degradation is also the reason why judgments based on SITA and ITPA frequently describe defendants as 'fallen women'. The Justice Ramaswamy bench in *Gaurav Jain vs Union of India & Ors* in 1997, for instance, makes frequent references to prostitutes as 'fallen women'. But, as Soneji is quick to point out, 'this narrative of the "fall" of devadasis from a Hindu golden age...[is] premised on little more than fantasy', and is a ploy both to target lower-caste women, and to represent wayward sexuality *as* a loss of caste. Repeatedly, amendments to the Madras Devadasi Act name lower castes as being in particular need of policing. The Andhra Pradesh Devadasis (Prohibition of Dedication) Act of 1988, for instance, names several Dalit groups like the Basavi and Jogini as being in need of reform and rehabilitation. And indeed, Dr Muthulakshmi Reddy's obsession with producing 'hygienic' Indian women was premised entirely on the casteist allocations of purity and dirt. The lower castes are 'dirty' and sexually licentious; therefore, they need to be cleaned and contained, even though their sexual containment will not allow these women any upward mobility in the oppressive rigidity of the caste system. However, for the abolitionists, outlawing devadasis would at least keep sex in its place of authenticity.

There were thus three interlinked fronts on which the legal war against devadasis and tawaifs was waged. The first involved the deification of the modern nation-state, in which prostitution was a historical blot. The second required the reification of marriage, which would tame itinerant female desire and make it meaningful. And the third insisted on the maintenance of caste which, along with sex, would protect the purity of the individual and community. Perhaps unsurprisingly, upper-caste women were at the forefront in demanding the passage of both SITA and the Madras Devadasi Act; they described prostitution both as a blot on the face of the nation, and an affront to the honour of women. But even more, in Madras State, both the largely upper-caste Congress party and the anti-Brahminical Self-Respect Movement joined hands in attacking prostitution. While Congress leaders saw prostitution as a primitive valorization of sex, Dalit activists followed B.R. Ambedkar in seeing prostitution as a historic wrong visited upon lower-caste women.

Caste persisted as an important factor even in the gharanas of the north, in Banaras and Lucknow, where it got enmeshed, if not with bodily hygiene, then with artistic purity (which it did in Madras too). The desire to purify singing and dancing went hand in hand with the insistence on removing it from the realm of sex. Indeed, the history of the anti-nautch movement is simultaneously a history of moralizing immoral traffic and leaching aesthetic movements to make them more palatable to modern India. As Jyotsna Bapat points out: 'The demand for the cultural tradition was an art form that was "morally" correct. Separating love from shringar or eroticism was the first step in the purification process. The erotic aspect of the dance form was dropped and the dance made chaste for the viewer.' This move towards chastity took place both in relation to Bharatanatyam, on the one hand, and Kathak, on the other. From south to north, modern India was united in its dismissal of immorality in culture. Suddenly, art forms that had been nurtured for generations by devadasis and tawaifs were forcibly shifted away from erotic practice to esoteric texts. The newly-classicized dance forms travelled a long distance from their non-conjugal devadasi and tawaif pasts to become means by which bourgeois young women make themselves more attractive on the marriage market.

Such a movement away from the devadasis and tawaifs stems directly from a legal loophole afforded by SITA that allowed professional women singers and dancers to perform so long as they did not indulge in prostitution. Among other things, this meant a formal separation between 'artistes' and 'prostitutes'. In relation to Banaras, Saba Dewan notes that 'many well-known kathak families had been successful in negotiating space for themselves within the nationalist project of an appropriately "classical" music culture. Their projection of an upper-caste status no doubt helped in gaining greater social acceptance from the votaries of Hindu nationalism', while Muslim accompanist musicians, seen as low-caste and outcasts 'had little choice but to either cast their lot with tawaifs or to give up music-making altogether'.

After having their professional work outlawed by a series of legislations, many women from devadasi and tawaif families migrated to big cities in order to find work as dancers in films, restaurants, clubs, and bars. But here too they were thwarted by the law. Perhaps the most shocking example of this was the Maharashtra government's ban in 2005 of dancing girls in bars that were otherwise allowed to remain open. In fact, the Bombay Police Act was amended to ban the dancers alone. The Supreme Court finally overturned the ban in 2019 on the grounds that it discriminated against Articles 14 and 15 of the Constitution guaranteeing equality and non-discrimination. It also upheld the argument that the ban on dancing girls violated Article 21 of the Constitution, which guarantees the Right to Livelihood. This was the same argument used by Husna Bai in 1958 to protect her right to work as a prostitute.

Even though the Supreme Court reversed the ban, it did so only fourteen years after it had come into effect. The delay in overturning the ban meant that the amendment to the Bombay Police Act succeeded in its goal of disbanding and impoverishing dancing women. Even worse, the social campaign in support of the ban had dredged up well-worn and ugly debates about the role of women in public. As with SITA and the Madras Devadasi Act, the active role in calling for the ban was taken by women who insisted, as Sameena Dalwai describes it, that 'women at home [need] the government's protection against women in the bars'. This wedge between Good vs Bad Women has always been exploited by the law in order to reinforce a moralistic paradigm of conjugal sexuality for women. The 'good' woman is married to one man while the 'bad' woman has sex with multiple men. Tellingly, in Dalwai's narrative, 'pro-ban campaigns circulated a poster that said, "Sweety or Savitri—Who are you with?"'

Who indeed? 'Sweety' as the unreliably honeyed vamp is pitted against the mythological 'Savitri' who rescues her husband even from the clutches of death. Sweety doesn't have an authentically 'Indian' name while Savitri is one of the founding pillars of Hindu womanhood. Sweety is financially independent while Savitri follows her husband around and serves his parents. So long as a woman is sexually and financially dependent on a man, all is well. In fact, this is a position the law states frequently. In its 1970 judgment in *Re: Devakumar & Ors vs Unknown*, the Madras High Court explicitly states that 'prostitution involves indiscriminate employment of a woman's body for hire. *Obviously*, it excludes intercourse which a person may have with a permanently kept concubine or with a woman without paying any consideration either in cash or in kind' (my emphasis). Immorality is immoral only when women get paid money by multiple men for sex.[12] These multiple payments, according to the Madras High Court, destroy the sanctity of sex. The law then takes it upon itself to discriminate against the indiscriminate lifestyle of prostitutes. They must be banned from performing sexual labour in the public sphere. They must not be allowed to infect the authenticity of sex with the commerce of money. They must be moral like SITA, not immoral like Sweety.

OBSCENE

If we want to learn about obscenity, then the law teaches us three inter-related lessons about it.

Lesson I: Demarcation

In 2006, several criminal charges of obscenity were filed under Sections 292 and 294 of the Indian Penal Code against world-renowned artist Maqbool Fida Husain. These charges were brought against Husain's famous painting 'Bharat Mata', which depicted India as a woman in distress, with the geography of the country mapped onto the contours of a woman's naked body. Obscenity charges were filed in Pandharpur in Maharashtra, Rajkot in Gujarat, and Indore and Bhopal in Madhya Pradesh. The then 90-year-old artist was required to run from pillar to post, summoned by different courts for hearings. The Supreme Court finally consolidated all these cases and referred them to the Delhi High Court, which ruled in 2008 in the artist's favour, declaring that his painting was not obscene. By this point, M.F. Husain had already been in self-imposed exile for two years, and he died in London three years later in 2011, unable to return to the land that he loved because he feared for his life at the hands of right-wing, anti-obscenity mobs.

Obscenity can be a matter of life and death. Despite this urgency, though, obscenity is also legally an unclear concept. In fact, a fundamental question in both anti-obscenity laws and obscenity judgments is what, *exactly*, counts as obscene? Famously, Justice Stewart of the US Supreme Court in 1964 defined obscenity by saying, 'I will know it when I see it.' But this assertion of certainty is based entirely on uncertainty. If obscenity can be known when it is seen, then does obscenity depend entirely on the opinion of the beholder? Is there anything objectively obscene about an act or book or painting on which everyone can agree? If I will know it when I see it, then does that mean I can potentially see obscenity anywhere?[1]

Reflecting this blurriness in his 2008 judgment vindicating M.F. Husain on charges of obscenity, Justice Sanjay Kishan Kaul asserted that 'Beauty lies in the eyes of the beholder and so does obscenity'. This lack of clarity opens up the realm of the obscene to unending charges of subjective bias. If the law is meant to *define* what it judges, then in the case of obscenity, the law fails. But if we cannot legally tell the difference between what is and what is not obscene, then how do we pass judgment?

Take, for example, the problem of differentiation articulated by the appellants in *Indian Hotel and Restaurant Association vs The State of Maharashtra & Ors.* Finally decided in 2017, the judgment in this case ruled against the Maharashtra government's 2005 ban on bar dancing. The appellants 'submitted that the [bar] dancers merely imitate the dance steps and movements of Hindi movie actresses. They wear traditional clothes such as ghagra cholis, sarees and salwar kameez. On the other hand, the actresses in movies wear revealing clothes: shorts, swimming costumes and revealing dresses'. So which one is obscene: the bar dancers or the movie actresses? Justice Sikri in this case moved to overturn the ban on bar dancers in Maharashtra. But the question posed by counsel remained unanswered: if two sets of actions are close to being identical, then on what basis might one be deemed obscene and the other one not? Even more, if the non-obscene set demonstrably wears fewer clothes, then what is the basis on which it has not been deemed obscene? What is the role of nudity in determining obscenity?

The most widely used legal response to this difficult question of demarcation is: context. Justice Kaul notes that 'one of the tests in relation to judging nude/semi-nude pictures of women as obscene is also a particular posture or pose or the surrounding circumstances which may render it to be obscene but in the present [Husain] painting...the contours of the woman's body represent nothing more than the boundaries/map of India. There can be a number of postures or poses that one can think of which can really stimulate a man's deepest hidden passions and desires [but this is not one of them]'. Even though the judgment exonerates the artist of charges of obscenity, it keeps tripping up on the question of the obscene itself. On what basis does Justice Kaul say that 'the contours of the woman's body represent nothing more than the boundaries/map of India'? Clearly, they represent much more to those who filed obscenity charges against Husain. And if this pose, despite its nudity, is an innocent one, then which are the poses that 'can really stimulate a man's deepest hidden passions and desires'? What is the distinction between these different poses? The judgment assumes that the answer will be uniform across all 'men'. But the very existence of the judgment—adjudicating a *dispute* about what is and is not obscene—witnesses otherwise.

These disputes extend from the visual image to the printed word and beyond. In *State vs Thakur Prasad & Ors* (1958), a bookseller and an author were charged with printing and writing obscene material; the book in question was titled *Asli Kokshastra*. In his judgment, Justice D. Roy asserts that 'anything calculated to inflame the passions is obscene'. He attempts to clarify even further that 'anything distinctly calculated to incite a reader to indulge in acts of indecency or immorality is obscene. A book may be obscene although it contains but a single obscene passage'. Distinct calculation implies intention and knowledge on the part of the artist, even though other obscenity judgments discount the question of knowledge altogether, saying prior knowledge is irrelevant to whether or not a book or a song or a painting conveys an effect of obscenity.

But perhaps more significantly, Justice Roy states that even a single passage is enough to condemn an entire book as obscene. What might such a passage look like? In *Asli Kokshastra*, there are some descriptions of oral sex, which are probably the passages to which the judge refers. But a writer like Saadat Hasan Manto—no stranger to charges of obscenity—complicates this notion of obscene language even further. 'There are few words that are obscene per se,' he claims. 'It is usage which can make the chastest of words obscene. I don't think anything is inherently obscene. However, even a chair or a cooking pot can become obscene if presented in such a way.' *Any* word can become an obscene word.[2] I will know it when I see it. Obscenity is both in the bedroom and the kitchen, everywhere and nowhere at once.

This lack of distinction between what is and is not obscene is written into the law itself. Section 292 of the IPC, which prohibits the sale of obscene books, provides an exception to its own reach: 'Exception: this section does not extend to any book, pamphlet, writing, drawing or painting kept or used bona fide for religious purposes or any representation sculptured, engraved, painted or otherwise represented, on or in any temple, or on any car used for the conveyance of idols, or kept or used for religious purposes.' Religion cannot be obscene, even and especially when it is explicitly sexual. According to this exception to the law, sex cannot be religious, which is patently untrue as a single glance at the *temples* of Khajuraho makes clear.

Different judgments attempt different kinds of demarcations. The 1965 judgment in *Ranjit D. Udeshi vs The State of Maharashtra*, for instance, tries to separate obscenity from pornography. It states confidently that 'there is, of course, some difference between obscenity and pornography in that the latter denotes writings, pictures etc. intended to arouse sexual desire while the former may include writings etc. not intended to do so but which have that tendency. Both, of course, offend against public decency and morals but pornography is obscenity in a more aggravated form'. So now obscenity is a matter of degree rather than kind? How do we separate un-obscene nudity from the obscene variety? When is sex obscene and when is it not? What kind of songs arouse sexual desire and which do not? In the M.F. Husain case, Justice Kaul struggles to bring some order to the avalanche of obscenity the respondents present to him. 'In so far as the scope of Section 292 is concerned,' he notes, 'it is clear that for an offence to be made out under the said section, its ingredients need to be met. In the context of the present painting, to be deemed to be obscene, it has to satisfy at least one of the three conditions: (i) if it is lascivious; (ii) it appeals to the prurient interest, and (iii) it tends to deprave and corrupt persons who are likely to read, see or hear the matter alleged to be obscene.' The most telling words in this section of the judgment are 'it is clear', since not one single word of the three 'conditions' laid down by the law to determine obscenity has, in fact, been defined. As Justice Harlan of the US Supreme Court observed in 1971, 'one man's vulgarity is another man's lyric'. No definition, no demarcation.

And so, Lesson #1: Obscenity fundamentally raises the problem of demarcation, of how to separate good depictions of sex from bad ones.

Lesson II: Containment

Statutes and judgments need to separate the not-obscene from the obscene in order to lay down the ambit of the law.[3] In the 1981 Andhra Pradesh High Court judgment in *3 Aces A Partnership Firm vs Commissioner of Police*, we see the framework within which such a legal demarcation can be made. Rejecting the plea by the owners of 3 Aces that they should be allowed to continue holding cabaret dances in their establishment, Justice P. Choudary notes that the legal prohibition is 'against the stripping of clothes and exposure of body by the cabaret dancers [and] is imposed not for the purpose of enforcing any morals but only for the purpose of maintenance of peace. The fact that private nude exhibitions are not banned under the above Act, appears to me to be conclusively against the petitioner... The type of public entertainments conducted in these places in the name of cabaret dances by exposure of female body draws in large numbers of those who are aesthetically desiccated, socially defiant, culturally deviant and psychologically despondent... The character and the composition of the crowd that gathers there is such'.

In this passage from the judgment, we get a malodorous whiff of what counts legally as obscene: it is a sexuality associated with the lower classes. In his breathtaking description of the men frequenting the cabarets as 'aesthetically desiccated, socially defiant, culturally deviant and psychologically despondent', Justice Choudary makes it clear that the masses are the

Pulp fiction covers. Reprinted with permission from Blaft Publications.

ones who are particularly susceptible to obscenity. Or rather, that what the masses enjoy is what qualifies as being obscene. The same dance performed in a 'private' exhibition for those who can afford it, would be fine. But when the audience is the great unwashed 'public', then it is unacceptable.[4] Masses cannot be contained within neat confines. The challenge for obscenity law is thus to prevent the spill-over of the masses into the (upper) classes. Justice Choudary is quite specific about the kinds of environments in which the 'female' body must not be exposed—they are ones that draw audiences in 'large numbers'.

This class stratification extends also to writers. In *State vs Thakur Prasad*, Justice Roy addresses the idea that eminent writers and stylistically complex texts might not necessarily be obscene. But, he adds, 'in the present case Ram Lagan Pandey does not and cannot claim to be an eminent writer, nor can it be said that the book in Hindi is composed in a style which is not easily understood by all. There can be no doubt that the book was written, printed and published and brought into circulation for prurient tastes'. Pulpy potboilers feed prurient public appetites, and commit the crime of what Charu Gupta terms 'providing eroticism to the masses'.

These masses and their desires need to be contained. Mass eroticism needs to be rendered ob-scene and kept offstage. This idea seems to be at the social core of obscenity. In the absence of a legal definition, it is this social understanding of obscenity that fills out the empty set of the obscene. The candidates in need of containment are multiple, but they inevitably involve the great unwashed masses and/or religious and gendered minorities. In all the cases examined thus far, the people accused of obscenity are either lower-class, or Muslims. Anyone who threatens the comfortable continuation of a hierarchy of social repression—Muslims, women, lower-class people—are typically the ones who are vilified in a majoritarian State for being 'too' sexual, and displaying a sexual appetite that needs to be contained. That the courts sometimes let them off speaks to the good sense of individual judges. But the system itself is heavily biased against these designated bearers of 'otherness'—the people rendered dirty by a bigoted State and obscene by a prejudiced populace. If obscenity law was imported into India by the sexually-puritanical British, then Indian casteism and communalism has led to its flourishing.

Writing about Hindi-language sex publications in Uttar Pradesh in the early twentieth century, Charu Gupta notes that for the upper classes, 'Shringar was acceptable if it belonged to a fantasy world or if it was restricted to the elite. The trouble with eroticism was that people in general wanted it and liked it, and it seemed to get everywhere. And the trouble with such mass eroticism was its subversion of the usual rules of order and propriety'. If obscenity is described in the law as something that is lascivious, prurient, depraved, and corrupt, then every one of these terms also gets class-coded. Despite not being defined, obscenity names a threat to the status-quo of gender, religion, and class. It overflows its socially prescribed bounds; as such, it needs to be contained once again within those boundaries.

A tale from 1890 gives a fascinating account of how the law's understanding of obscenity is tied to the containment of popular desire. 'When several editors of Moradabad were convicted and fined on the charge [of publishing obscene advertisements for aphrodisiacs],' Gupta notes, 'some of them...argued that the advertisements were not published to encourage immorality or outrage the public decency but were intended for the public good. "Obscene" words, after all, were to be found even in legal and medical works.'

The publishers were both right and wrong. 'Obscene' words for which their publications were indicted are indeed to be found in legal and medical books. But when those words are found there, they are not termed obscene. No one, as far as I know, has ever filed a criminal complaint against writers of legal handbooks or medical textbooks that are used in law and medical schools. Because if it exists in highly-educated settings, if its milieu is upper-class, if its audience is wealthy, then sex becomes science. When it is widely available on footpaths and railway stations, then sex becomes crass and obscene. Thus, 'high art' is not often convicted for obscenity. In a strange way, this upper-class bias might have been responsible for the dismissal of the charges of obscenity against M.F. Husain, even as his religion was what invited the charges in the first place.

This class bias is also why the ban on bar dancers, the frequent closure of cabarets, the incessant pursuit of pulp readers, have ongoing lives. All these categories of people threaten to contaminate a deeply hierarchical social structure. In response to the threat of contamination, the law suggests containment. Or, in the parlance of the Covid pandemic, the law suggests that the obscene masses need to be put in containment zones.

And therefore, Lesson #2: Obscenity is a problem of containment. It names a threat to sexual and social boundaries that allegedly seeps out of the lower classes, gendered and religious minorities.

Lesson III: Redemption

In *Ranjit D. Udeshi vs State of Maharashtra*, a five-member Supreme Court bench deliberated on the question of whether or not D.H. Lawrence's novel, *Lady Chatterley's Lover,* was obscene. The novel is about a failed marriage between two upper-class people, and the deeply satisfying sexual relationship between the upper-class employer and her lower-class gardener. D.H. Lawrence presents us with a scenario that breaches both social and sexual taboos; it should come as no surprise, therefore, that the judges of the Supreme Court found that the novel was indeed obscene. By introducing the lower classes into the scene of sex, the novel guaranteed its own obscenity. Accordingly, the judgment sought to contain the spread of obscene sex.

But the Court could hardly come out and admit openly to its class bias or its sexual prudery (a prudery that is heightened when it involves, as it does in the novel, a woman's sexual pleasure). Instead, it found a language with which to describe the book that has now become standard in the law's encounters with obscenity. Upholding the verdict punishing the Bombay booksellers for selling unexpurgated copies of *Lady Chatterley's Lover*, the Supreme Court noted that 'Obscenity without a preponderating social purpose or profit cannot have the Constitutional protection of free speech or expression'. The bookstore selling the book was called the Happy Book Stall, but alas, its happiness did not last long in light of the legal version of acceptable sex.

In 1969, Section 292 of the IPC was amended so that the publication of sexual matter could be justified if it was in the public good, 'in the interest of science, literature, art or learning or other objects of general concern'. In this version, sex must be fully clothed, preferably in a married heterosexual relationship, and holding a child. There is to be no talk of sexual pleasure, especially for a woman, and no hint of social disturbance. Even better, such a scenario might feature an image or a song communicating the dangers of sex, attempting to educate the masses about what counts as good sex and what should definitely be rejected as bad sex.

Sex has therefore to justify itself as being for the greater good before the law will allow its free expression. But, as we have already seen, the greater good does not indicate greater numbers or the general populace. Rather, it denotes refinement—greater in terms of class rather than size. Sex that is popular rather than esoteric, carnal rather than sublimated, widespread rather than contained, is the danger that obscenity laws seek to chasten. The M.F. Husain judgment, for instance, quoting *Udeshi*, makes it clear that 'where obscenity and art are mixed, art must be so preponderating as to throw obscenity into shadow or render the obscenity so trivial and insignificant that it can have no effect and can be overlooked'.

This legal observation also raises a different question: is *some* obscenity alright or is *all* obscenity always bad? Justice Kaul notes that if the artistic merit of the piece is great enough, then we can ignore the obscenity by brushing it under the carpet or, in his words, by pushing it into the shadows. So does the law not punish all obscenity? Is there a distinction between good and bad obscenity? And what, in this regard, is the relation between the obscene and the sexual?

The *Udeshi* judgment is useful with regard to this question, especially when it states that 'the mere treating with sex and nudity in art and literature is not per se evidence of obscenity'. While the obscene and the sexual might overlap in some areas, they do not fully map onto one another. The judgment, crucially, says that the Constitution can protect *some* kinds of sex and nudity, but it is unclear about which nudity is protected and which is not. And then, attempting the hoary legal tradition of trying to define the obscene, the judges state that 'obscenity is treating with sex in a manner appealing to the carnal side of human nature or having that tendency'. The obscene is always sexual but not all sex is obscene.

Far from defining it, however, this statement confuses the issue of obscenity even further. The *Udeshi* judgment says specifically that sex must *not* appeal to carnal desire in order to be publicly permitted. But what should sex do if it does not appeal to 'the carnal side of human nature'? Carnality is the recognition of the physicality of sex, and the body's sexual needs. By explicitly saying that sex must not appeal to our carnal side, the judgment says that sex must not be sexual if it is to be legally protected. It must be esoteric and refined away from the body. So what should sex do once it is divorced from our carnal needs? Hang out at religious places of worship? Go to school? Make a documentary film? In fact, sex does appear in all these places, so how do we determine where and which sex appeals to our carnal desires? The most chaste religious icon might appeal to 'the carnal side of human nature'. The most scientific syllabus might excite the passions. The most hard-hitting documentary on poverty might be labelled 'pornographic' because people derive pleasure from it. So when is it alright for sex to be seen, and when is it obscene—can the law actually adjudicate at what point any given situation will cross the line from sanctity to carnality? According to *Udeshi*, obscenity is sex that is sexy. Dull and unappealing sex is not legally considered obscene. And even more, non-obscene sex is sex that can be appropriated as social service.

In the *3 Aces* judgment banning cabaret dancing, Justice Choudary drives home this point. In order to 'earn the high appellation of free speech and to deserve the sanctimoniously appropriate constitutional protection', he states, 'the act in question must, in some measure or degree, be an expositor of ideas, thoughts or feelings... In a particular context, exposure of the body associated with an expression of a feeling or an idea may or may not be regarded as "obscene". But it can be said without fear of contradiction that an elemental act of baring the female breasts and stripping clothes that cover private parts indulged in as done in these cabaret dances without ever being touched up at any stage by the rhythmic beauty of context or resonance of exposition is utter vulgarity without any socially redeeming quality in it'. Sex without art can only be seen as an appeal to carnality. Sex must specifically turn our attention away from the body if is to escape the tag of obscenity. It must be cerebral, emotional, or artistic—it cannot be carnal.[5]

Consolidating and extending what the *Udeshi* and *Husain* judgments say, the *3 Aces* judgment insists that in order not to be obscene, sex needs to be (a) emotional, (b) socially useful, and (c) artistic. Unless sex can be immersed in rarefied realms, divorced from the vagaries of the body, and separated from the vicissitudes of the masses, it will be obscene. Unless sex is not sex, it will be obscene. In terms of Catholic morality, sex must be a utilitarian activity leading to social and sexual reproduction. If sex is treated as pleasurable, as a carnal need, as conducing to pleasure for its own sake—all of which are central tenets of a text like the *Kamasutra*—then all bets are off, and the obscenity laws have an opening in which to swoop in. Sex for the sake of sex, without preponderating social value, must be criminalized. As Charu Gupta observes, 'As soon as sexual descriptions celebrate desire and eroticism for their own sake, they become unacceptable and obscene.'

And so, Lesson #3: Obscenity must cover itself with social value in order to be redeemed. Sex that is pleasurably sexy rather than socially useful is deemed obscene.

~

These three lessons point to a larger problem that the law has with sex. The law is squeamish about sexual pleasure, especially of the popular variety. And it is repulsed by having to deal with pleasures of the body. The only sex acceptable to the law is non-carnal sex. But since non-carnal sex is an impossibility, all sex is potentially obscene.[6] Law encourages us to imagine an ideal world of good sex *versus* a fallen underworld of bad sex. But not a single law or judgment on obscenity has been able to draw this distinction convincingly. No matter how often it intones that obscenity and sex are not the same thing, then, for the law, that separation cannot be fathomed.[7] Legally, it is impossible to separate sex from obscenity. If the obscene is carnal, prurient, and vulgar, then it is so only because *sex is so*.

But instead of condemning sex outright, the law makes obscenity take the fall for the disturbing potential of sex. In law, arousal is obscene while modesty is good sex. Carnality is obscene while emotions are good sex. Popularity is obscene while secrecy is good sex. Boundary-breaking is obscene while social respect is good sex. Pleasure is obscene while reproduction is good sex. This is how the law makes us think of sex—it must be demure, sanctioned, emotional, and not physically arousing. Anything else is obscene. This is the zeitgeist of sex in India today, courtesy of the obscenity laws.

Coda

The last word belongs to the law. In July 2020, the Supreme Court echoed the Kerala High Court in refusing anticipatory bail to well-known activist Rehana Fathima in *Fathima A.S. vs State of Kerala*. Her 'crime' is that she asked her children—a boy aged fourteen and a girl aged eight—to paint on her naked torso. She then uploaded the video on YouTube, accompanied by a manifesto about unrealistic expectations around women's bodies and the need for urgent and open conversations about sex education. The post was titled 'Body Art and Politics'. Among the laws invoked in the case against her were the Protection of Children from Sexual Offences Act of 2012, and the Information Technology Act of 2000.

But the real legal question was about obscenity.

The Kerala High Court did not comment in much detail on the issue of obscenity, saying it would leave that determination to the investigating officer. But the judge couldn't resist recording his disapproval about activities that should have stayed within 'the four walls of her house' rather than emerging into the public sphere. Once the video sees the light of day, it becomes clear to the judge that 'the children are represented in the video uploaded in an indecent and obscene manner... painting on a naked body of their mother'. He then goes on censoriously to quote the *Manusmriti* on the rights and responsibilities of a mother.

The Supreme Court bench went even further. 'Why do you do all this?' asked an irritated Justice Arun Mishra of Rehana Fathima. 'You might be an activist but why do this? What kind of nonsense is this? It is obscenity clearly which you are spreading. It will leave the society in a very bad taste.'

Where does this bad taste come from and of what does it consist? Rehana Fathima is a well-known feminist who had in 2018 attempted to enter the Sabarimala temple, defying the temple's ban on the entry of menstruating women. In her recent video, she makes a point about taking seriously the physical and social realities of the female body. She has said that with her art experiment, she wanted to 'normalize the female form for her children and not allow distorted ideas of sexualization to pervade their minds'. Both menstruation and open conversations about sex are socially taboo in India today, and the laws attempting to reverse these taboos have all failed.

In such a climate, *Fathima A.S. vs State of Kerala* has waded into an entire cocktail of issues plaguing the country. As a part of her petition for anticipatory bail to the Supreme Court, Fathima noted that, historically, idols of goddesses in India appear with bare breasts, but when 'one prays at the temple the feeling is not of sexual arousal but one of divinity'. Even though she is potentially underestimating the reach of sexual desire by suggesting its non-existence in a sacred space, Fathima's claim was an attempt to describe the salutary effects of naturalizing naked torsos. This comparison of her own naked torso with those of Hindu goddesses immediately drew the ire of Hindutva groups who have accused her of obscenity. A Muslim artist targeted by right-wing Hindu organizations for an assertion of pan-religious affinities? Rehana Fathima's case brings to mind M.F. Husain, who too was hounded for his paintings of nude figures drawn from Hindu mythology. Both artists are prosecuted by laws under which goddesses—whether semi or fully nude—cannot legally be obscene, while human nudity is considered prurient and depraved.[8] The 'bad taste' to which Justice Mishra refers can only be generated by public displays of sex by gendered and religious minorities.

Rehana Fathima has very publicly disturbed categories of what counts as good and bad nudity. Her art has questioned the line spuriously drawn between art and sex. She has dared to talk about the female body and its forced association with sexual shame. She has laid bare difficult questions about the public and private nature of sex. To prosecute her for all these 'crimes', the right-wing's weapon of choice is the law against obscenity.

UNNATURAL

In order to wield their power, laws of desire depend on the moral opprobrium attached to the category of the 'unnatural'. The category itself is an empty space that can be filled with whatever the law sees fit, and it depends on terms like 'custom', 'nature', 'impurity', to bolster its power. Legal language in penal codes and judgments suggests that what the law considers 'unnatural' are desires and bodies that are transgendered, adulterous, menstruating, and homosexual.

I: Transgendered

'Call me Pinki Papa.'

With this hypothetical sentence addressed to her lover's daughter, athlete Pinki Pramanik raised several difficulties for law and society. She confounded gender difference by identifying as a woman yet asking to occupy a masculine category. She associated that masculine category not just with the colour pink, but also with the diminutive 'pinky'. And she asked to occupy the paternal role, which sits at the very top of the patriarchal food chain. The cherry on the cake was that Pinki Papa (which is what her girlfriend's daughter did in fact call her) was accused by her lover of rape. But in Indian law, rape is a crime that can only be perpetrated by a man against a woman.

The entire case against Pinki Pramanik thus hinged on whether she was a man or a woman. For the law, it was imperative to ascertain that fact, but sadly, the medical profession was unable to oblige. Teams of doctors, consisting of gynaecologists, radiologists, and other specialists at the SSKM Hospital in Kolkata, found it difficult to determine Pinki's sex. They declared her to be a male pseudo hermaphrodite (MPH) with 46,XY chromosome disorder of sexual development (DSD), in which a male chromosomal pattern of X and Y in each cell does not result in the full development of male genitalia. The team of medical experts arrived at the conclusion that Pinki was 'incapable of performing sexual intercourse like...an adult male in the ordinary course of nature'.

The ordinary course of nature. A court of law needs to know what the ordinary course of nature is in order to determine whether or not a person brought before them can be termed 'natural'. And in turn, whether the acts performed by this person are in keeping with, or against the order of, nature. A star athlete who had won several medals in female track events at national and international sports meets (Silver in the 2006 Commonwealth Games, Gold in the 2006 Asian Games), Pinki Pramanik was brought before the Calcutta High Court in 2014 on several charges, prime among them being rape (Sections 375 and 376 IPC), and deceitful cohabitation (Section 493 IPC). The adjudication of all these charges depended on determining what Pinki's sex was. Naturally.

After hearing forceful arguments on both sides, Justice Subrata Talukdar used the medical evidence as the basis on which to dismiss all charges against Pinki. Since her sex was medically indeterminate, she could not be classified as a man. And if she could not be classified as a man—a classification based entirely on the existence of a penis and testicles—then legally, she cannot be guilty of rape. Not guilty, then, under Sections 375 and 376 IPC. And also, therefore, not guilty under 493 IPC on charges of false promises and deceitful cohabitation. The judge reasoned that the complainant could have believed *either* that Pinki was a man and would marry her *or* that she was a woman and would never be able to marry her. If she believed that Pinki was a man, then the complainant would also have known that they couldn't get married because the complainant was married to someone else. And if the complainant believed that Pinki was a woman, then she wouldn't have been able to marry her anyway under the country's marriage laws (since such a marriage would be considered against the order of nature). Basing his verdict on the absence of a penis, then, the judge pronounced Pinki not guilty, though he stopped short of declaring her a woman. An interesting judgment in relation to a fe/male Pinki, whose father and mother, Durga and Pushpa, both have women's names.

As this case suggests, sports is the arena in which the question of what counts as a 'natural' body often arises. Like Pinki Pramanik in India, Caster Semenya in South Africa has been castigated for her DSD, and recently, disallowed by the Court of Arbitration for Sport from competing in any races between 400 metres and a mile. Semenya has refused to take drugs to lower her testosterone levels: her argument against the adjudication of what constitutes a naturally female body itself relies on the language of nature. 'I am very disappointed by this ruling, but refuse to let World Athletics drug me or stop me from being who I am. Excluding female athletes or endangering our health solely because of our natural abilities puts World Athletics on the wrong side of history,' she asserted. The question Caster Semenya raises is crucial for the law: are all bodies natural, or are only those bodies considered natural that conform to a prefabricated hormonal design (which is often achieved only by a course of artificial hormones)?

In India, perhaps the most significant advance in thinking about gender and its relation to the realm of the 'natural' came in the form of the Supreme Court judgment in *National Legal Services Authority vs Union of India & Ors* in 2014. In addition to mandating legal recognition of transgender people—including in the provision of education, health services, and job opportunities—the *NALSA* judgment insisted that 'transgender persons may be afforded the right of choice to determine whether to opt for male, female or transgender classification'. This means that in addition to creating a third category to accommodate people who might consider themselves neither male nor female, the Supreme Court also opened the door for transgender people to identify *as* male or female if they so desired. 'Self-identified gender can be either male or female or a third gender,' the Court insisted, adding that it preferred 'to follow the psyche of the person in determining sex and gender', adverting to 'the "Psychological Test" instead of the "Biological Test"'.

NALSA goes well beyond the physiological and insists that a transgendered person can *opt* to be a woman or a man, if they so desire. 'Any insistence on SRS [sex reassignment surgery] for declaring one's gender is immoral and illegal,' the Supreme Court bravely declared, standing by its decision that gender should be psychologically rather than physiologically determined, and that too, by the individual themselves.[1] But despite having been passed a few months before the Pinki Pramanik judgment, no one asked Pinki what sex she identified as. Instead, the judge relied on the medical report of an under-formed penis to disallow the charge of rape.

Meanwhile, the *NALSA* judgment had suspended the framing narrative of what makes a body 'natural' by asserting that we can decide our own nature. But the Transgender Persons (Protection of Rights) Act of 2019, allegedly based on the *NALSA* judgment, obfuscates the issue of self-determination of gender. It presumes instead that if a transgendered person wants to be identified as a man or a woman, then they will have to undergo SRS. All people who want to change their gender or identify as transgender need to have their desires vetted, screened, and approved by the district magistrate who can ask them to submit documentation to prove their gendered identity. The Act has moved beyond 'psychological' and 'biological' tests to legal and administrative ones. As always, we can only be the gender that the law says we are because the law tells us what our bodies 'naturally' are: 'The District Magistrate shall, on receipt of an application along with the certificate issued by the Medical Superintendent or Chief Medical Officer, and on being satisfied with the correctness of such certificate, issue a certificate indicating change in gender in such form and manner and within such time, as may be prescribed.' A certificate for a certificate for a 'correct' gender.

Interestingly, the Transgender Persons (Protection of Rights) Rules, 2020, undoes in part what the Act prohibits. Under the new Rules, transgender people can self-identify as such without needing to undergo a physical examination. There is no requirement for surgery in order to identify as male or female (applicants will still have to undergo a 'medical' procedure, but such a procedure could include psychotherapy). All processes, however, will still need to go through a district magistrate. The gaze of the law—even the relatively benevolent gaze of the Rules—continues to reveal gender as an administrative fiction. And it is a fiction that everywhere informs the law's attitude about the nature of bodies.

But the real question posed by *NALSA* is: will the law be able to give up its attachment to the idea of natural bodies? And if it does, then what will follow in its wake? The *NALSA* judgment could have a significant impact on several existing criminal laws that are based on gender—Sections 375 and 376 on rape prime among them. Pinki Pramanik's self-identification as a woman, backed by the medical report on her under-formed penis, prevented her from being convicted of rape under the current rape laws. But, post *NALSA*, a person identifying as male could be convicted of rape by virtue of that self-identification, whether or not he has a penis. In fact, even now, Section 375 of the Criminal Procedure Code provides for this possibility in its definition of rape, which includes the insertion of '*any object* or a part of the body, not being the penis, into the vagina, the urethra or anus of a woman' (my emphasis). Even a female body with XY chromosomes—currently deemed 'unnatural' on account of under-developed male genitalia—can insert an object into an orifice. If gender is to be self-identified, then presumably the absence of a penis will not protect one from the charge of rape.

Such a denaturing of the human body will also have a significant impact on civil laws, indeed on any law that assumes gender as the baseline for welfare schemes, reservations, etc. If carried out fully, this denaturing will revolutionize the law of desire.

However, until the revolution comes, nothing can stop the legal fiction of gender from defining natural and unnatural bodies. Thus it is that in *Faizan Siddiqui vs Sashastra Seema Bal* in 2011, the border security force rejected the plaintiff, Faizan Siddiqui, from recruitment at the rank of Constable. The doctor for the SSB stated that: 'Ms Faizan Siddiqui has undergone surgery for removal of testes followed by vaginoplasty. She will have to remain on female hormones life long and she

Pride paraders and taxi driver, Kolkata 2018.
Photo credit: Arpan.basuchowdhury on Wikimedia Commons
(See https://commons.wikimedia.org/wiki/
File:ABC_8909.jpg).

may remain disease free as long as she is compliant to medication. Although she may have a normal married life yet she will not be able to bear children in the natural way which may lead to adjustment problems in later life.' The natural female body is one that does not require supplementary medication to support its femininity, and which is able to bear children naturally. Women who cannot have children are not natural women. Women who have marital difficulties are not natural women. Women who need medical help to maintain pre-determined hormonal levels are not natural women. Faizan was refused the chance to become a Constable because her state of mind was mapped onto the state of her body and both were declared to be uncertain. The two judges in the Delhi High Court who heard the case in 2011 delivered a verdict in favour of Faizan's desire to join the border force as a woman constable. But the force of the doctor's conviction about what counts as natural gender continues to inform the law in 2020. Thus it is that even the new rules create no space for someone like Pinki Pramanik—a woman who wants to be called 'papa'. Such a desire is still not considered natural.

II: Adulterated

Let us move now from Pinki to Pinky.

During the hearings in *Joseph Shine vs Union of India* in 2018, Additional Solicitor General of India Pinky Anand stated the case for why the government opposed the repeal of Section 497 IPC, the section that criminalizes adultery.[2] In a concurring judgment striking down 497 as being violative of Articles 14, 15, and 21 of the Constitution, Justice Indu Malhotra summarized the case put forward by the ASG:

> Ms. Pinky Anand, learned ASG, forcefully submitted that adultery must be retained as a criminal offence in the I.P.C. She based her argument on the fact that adultery has the effect of breaking up the family which is the fundamental unit in society. Adultery is undoubtedly morally abhorrent in marriage, and no less an offence than the offences of battery, or assault. By deterring individuals from engaging in conduct

> which is potentially harmful to a marital relationship, Section 497 is protecting the institution of marriage, and promoting social well-being.
>
> The Respondents submit that an act which outrages the morality of society, and harms its members, ought to be punished as a crime. Adultery falls squarely within this definition.
>
> The learned ASG further submitted that adultery is not an act that merely affects just two people; it has an impact on the aggrieved spouse, children, as well as society. Any affront to the marital bond is an affront to the society at large. The act of adultery affects the matrimonial rights of the spouse, and causes substantial mental injury.
>
> Adultery is essentially violence perpetrated by an outsider, with complete knowledge and intention, on the family which is the basic unit of a society.

The Union of India lost the case, and adultery was decriminalized by the Supreme Court in 2018. In *Joseph Shine*, the judges tried to stamp out the inherent sexism of Section 497—the law did not give a wife the right to sue her husband or his (female) lover for infidelity, and also made the wife immune from such prosecution. In being thus formulated, Section 497 ignored the fact that women too have sexual desires and act on them. Instead, it made all such desire subservient to what the husband might want, which in turn was considered synonymous with what was best for society.

In opposition to this assumption, the *Joseph Shine* judgment insisted that women need to be given a voice in determining the sexual politics of a marriage:

'Not only is there a denial of sexual agency [in Section 497], but women are also not seen to be harmed by the offence. Thus, the provision is not simply about protecting the sanctity of the marital relationship. It is all about protecting a husband's interest in his "exclusive access to his wife's sexuality".' Even more, the judgment added, 'the legislature has, while ostensibly protecting the sanctity of marriage, invaded the dignity of women'. While the legal blow against sexism is very welcome, the *Joseph Shine* verdict needed to more rigorously examine two crucial ideas that fuel the social horror of adultery, and which continue to be operative despite the court's decriminalization of Section 497.

The first is the shared emphasis, both by the law and the overturning of the law, on the sanctity of marriage. The law includes its provisions against adultery in Chapter XX of the Penal Code—'Of Offences Relating to Marriage'. Earlier challenges to 497 were dismissed because judges stated that 'the stability of marriage is not an ideal to be scorned'. Pinky Anand's challenge to *Joseph Shine* harps on the desirability of marriage. And the judgment in *Joseph Shine* too speaks repeatedly of the need to 'preserve the institution of marriage'. Marriage is seen by the law as a binding agent for desire, and loosening it can be catastrophic.[3] Marriage is considered to be a social and moral ideal, even as the judgment tries to make it more equitable between husband and wife.[4]

Second, *Joseph Shine* takes as its mandate the fact that Section 497 pays no heed to women's desire, when it should. Based on this missing term, the judges arrive at the conclusion that the adultery law ignores women. And they take up cudgels on women's behalf to bring their desire too within the ambit of marriage and sex. But the omission in 497 is not because the law does not consider the question of women's sexuality. Quite the opposite. Not mentioning women's sexuality in 497 is akin to not mentioning the word 'homosexual' in Section 377. From Blackstone to Macaulay, our colonial masters have very clearly approached the law in this manner: Do not name the desires whose existence you do not want to acknowledge. Even mentioning such desire will conjure it into being, and then it will be difficult to put the genie back in the bottle.

Far from ignoring women, then, the law's misogyny stems from its assumption that adultery is always about women's desire. Women are the ones who can *adulterate* the family bloodline by having sex outside wedlock. The reason why an unmarried woman having an affair with a married man is not criminalized by Section 497, for instance, is because there is no man who is threatened by adulteration in such a scenario. But a married woman having an affair with another man directly threatens the purity of the husband's lineage. While men always need to stamp their offspring—hence the tradition of the surname or the sir's name—it is women who threaten the authenticity of that stamp. This is why adultery becomes a crime against a man (performed by a woman). The law on adultery might not have mentioned women, but it is about women. Adultery is everywhere marked in relation to the woman's body and its allegedly unreliable desires. Even as *Joseph Shine* argued forcefully against the absence of women's sexuality in the law on adultery, it needed to pay more attention to the ubiquitous *presence* of women's sexuality in our thinking about adultery. Overturning the law on adultery as a means of respecting women's sexuality ignores ongoing social narratives about the specifically female threat of adulteration. This is the version of misogyny that *Joseph Shine* should have tackled more fully: not that women's sexuality is often ignored, but that women's sexuality is always considered impure.

Adultery is understood as a threat to familial and social purity—defined by and for men—by the marauding desires of a lascivious woman. This is made clear in the famous judgment in *K.M. Nanavati vs State of Maharashtra* in 1961, where the Bombay High Court 'present[ed] the commonplace problem of an alleged murder by an enraged husband of a paramour of his wife'. Murderousness between men as a consequence of a woman's unreliable desire is *commonplace*. Indeed, it becomes the most notable fact of an adultery case. However, all the relationships in this sentence—husband and paramour—revolve around the woman, whose desire is central to the scenario rather than being absent from it.

Later on, the judgment summarizes the events of the Nanavati affair: 'From the consideration of the entire evidence the following facts emerge: The deceased seduced the wife of the accused. She had confessed to him of her illicit intimacy with the deceased. It was *natural* that the accused was enraged at the conduct of the deceased and had, therefore, sufficient motive to do away with the deceased' (my emphasis). Some things the law takes to be absolutely natural: that (a) women will be sexually unreliable; and (b) men will be murderously enraged. The assumption about women's untrustworthy desires is fundamental to this and all cases of adultery. But the further question is whether women are helpless seducees or scheming seductresses. Has the woman been fooled into having an affair—the trope of the foolish and unwitting woman has been marshalled, most recently, in accusations of 'love jihad'—or has she actively seduced her lover?

In her work on the Nanavati case (a case that led eventually to the demise of the jury system in India), Bachi Karkaria notes that: 'Through the initial Sessions court murder trial by jury, Kawas' legion of worshippers cast him as Lord Rama enjoined by his dharma to slay Ravana, who had abducted his innocent wife. The editor of *Blitz*, Russy Karanjia, drew this analogy frontally. The defence team did it more obliquely, presenting Kawas as the ideal man: a decorated naval officer away at sea for months in the service of the country, forced to leave his wife vulnerable to the machinations of an evil man with no patriotism on his CV.'

Even though the woman had been openly and polyamorously sexual, she was also recuperated by the defence as naïve. These are the two sharply contrasting responses to Sylvia Nanavati, née King, that Karkaria points to: 'While the defence team painted a picture of

TRAGEDY OF THE ETERNAL TRIANGLE

SYLVIA NANAVATI TELLS HER

STORY OF LOVE AND TORTURE

BLITZ

ASIA'S FOREMOST NEWSMAGAZINE

EVERY SATURDAY

ALL THIS & A SKULL TOO!

Is your husband a good provider?

Gluco

BISCUITS

Death Rattle of Bandung: P. 3

Image from *Blitz* newsmagazine, October 17, 1959.
Reprinted with permission from Rita Mehta.

blamelessness, the hysterical crowds outside the court defamed her. They accused her of being a "typical" amoral, sex-hungry foreigner jumping into an adulterous bed with no thought of her valiant husband sailing the seas in defence of the nation, and no care for the children neglected because of her uncontrolled desires. She was even reportedly spat upon.'

Do women have 'uncontrolled desires' or are they 'innocent and vulnerable'? Neither society nor the law has ever been able to settle this question. Perhaps because both questions are versions of one another. And both versions require that women be kept an eye on, either to save them from themselves, in the first instance, or to save them from others, in the second instance. Either way, women's desires must be controlled if they are to be prevented from fulfilling their destiny as agents of adulteration. This fear of female desire has haunted patriarchal societies for centuries. And *Joseph Shine*'s recognition that women too can be adulterers is not going to conjure away that fear. In fact, it might well do the opposite. For the law, the fundamental 'victim' of adultery is marriage. And marriage must be retained—even in the *Joseph Shine* judgment—as the bedrock of society. It is this compulsion to retain the reliability of marriage and prevent it from adulteration that leads to violence—either against the individual in the case of Kawas Nanavati murdering (the aptly named) Prem Ahuja, or mythically in the case of Rama murdering Ravana.[5]

In her concurring judgment in *Joseph Shine*, Justice

Indu Malhotra states that the 'historical background in which Section 497 was framed is no longer relevant in contemporary society'. Is that really the case? To take just one instance that suggests the opposite, let us look at the Indian Penal Code (Amendment) Bill, 2019—a Private Member's Bill submitted by Jagdambika Pal (a member of the ruling Bharatiya Janata Party). The Bill suggests that Section 497 should be retained and rewritten as follows:

> 497. Whoever has illicit and immoral relationship with a person who is and whom he knows or has reason to believe to be the spouse of another person, such illicit and immoral relationship not amounting to any other offence under this code, is guilty of the offence of adultery, and shall be punished with imprisonment of either description for a term which may extend up to five years, or with fine, or with both.

Despite the use of the male pronoun, Mr Pal's proposed amendment levels the playing field for men and women, and makes the crime of adultery gender-neutral. His rationale for this amendment is the same as that of *Joseph Shine*: 'The object of section 497 of Indian Penal Code, 1860, was to preserve the sanctity of marriage as society abhors marital infidelity. According to Indian culture, marriage is considered sacred, and mutual fidelity and devotion to partners are still considered to be the essence of marriage.' The sanctity of marriage (an institution that is always unequal for women), the code of monogamy, and the need to be gender-neutral in the law have all been upheld in this proposal. Indeed, they have all been reinforced. But this rationale—which does not deviate from the letter of *Joseph Shine*—is proposed in order to *retain* the criminal status of 497. Clearly, making a law gender-neutral does not itself strike at the root of patriarchal assumptions about men and women. And it does not do away with the noxious gendered expectations embedded within the institution of marriage itself.

The BJP government, of which Jagdambika Pal is a member, and in which Pinky Anand was an ASG until May 2020, has clearly understood desire to be an adulteration caused by, and associated with, women. The question about whether women are naturally pure or adulterated tends to favour the latter option. The story of Rama and Sita too, we remember, ends with Sita paying the price of suspected adulteration. This is because the threat of adulteration in marriage is a self-fulfilling prophecy, premised as it is on the requirement of female purity. It is precisely the widespread expectation that women should be virginal and sexually pure that leads to the conviction they are adulterated. By upholding the sanctity of marriage, *Joseph Shine* ignores this misogynistic ether in which 497 is drenched, and ends up reinforcing the law's sexism, however inadvertently, and despite its good intentions. So long as we hold marriage in high regard, it is always going to be women's desires that are under the microscope, whether or not women themselves are mentioned in the law.

III: Menstruating

As just one example of how suspect women's desires are in law and society, let us consider the Sabarimala judgment, which was delivered in the same year—2018—as *Joseph Shine*. The verdict in *Indian Young Lawyers Association vs State of Kerala* held by a 4:1 majority that it is illegal for the Ayyappan temple in Sabarimala to prohibit women aged 10–50 years from entering the temple.[6] The case pivoted around discriminations encapsulated in Rule 3(b) of the Kerala Hindu Places of Public Worship (Authorisation of Entry) Rules of 1965, which state that 'Women at such time during which they are not by custom and usage allowed to enter a place of worship' will not be allowed into the temple. Without explicitly naming menstruation as the reason for its discriminatory attitude, the rules refer to the 'custom' by which menstruating women are considered impure and unclean, and on the basis of which they are prohibited from pursuing a range of activities, including eating food with other members of the household. But euphemisms about being unclean and impure cover over the real cause of horror, which is that menstruating women are also considered to be sexually active women.

As such, since the deity at Sabarimala is considered to be celibate, the thinking is that he must not be exposed to sexually active women who might seduce him into a sexual relationship.[7] The presumption here is of heterosexuality. A male god will be sexually tempted by sexually-active female devotees. Quite apart from conjuring a scenario of sleaziness, this assumption of heterosexuality has never once been questioned as a *legal* assumption. Instead, menstruating women are quite easily made synonymous in court with scheming designs against celibate men (and gods). The very presence of female bodies is considered to be both adulterated and adulterating. Women's desires seem designed to interrupt the pious activities of men. Their sexuality is tied to who they 'naturally' are—people who menstruate—and thus women's very nature is used against them. They are naturally unnatural.

Reprinted with the permission of Alok Nirantar.

Heterosexuality, then, is the 'natural' assumption of the law, as is the sexually polluting nature of women. Indeed, so widespread is this assumption, that over fifty review petitions were filed against the Sabarimala judgment, insisting that women should be kept out of holy places. In November 2019, a five-judge bench of the Supreme Court headed by Chief Justice of India Ranjan Gogoi ruled that the question of the entry of women into places of worship is not restricted to the Sabarimala temple alone, and must be considered in relation to other religious places as well.[8] The Court thus decided to refer this larger question to a seven-judge bench.

As a consequence of this referral to a larger bench, and despite the fact that the verdict allowing women entry into the temple still stands until it is overturned, the priests and officials of Sabarimala stop women of menstruating age from entering the temple. The Supreme Court's commitment to constitutional morality seems weak in the face of patriarchal impunity against female impurity: the 2018 judgment is being flouted every single day, with no consequences. The very touchability of the female body in a heterosexist framework renders it, in a case of twisted logic, as untouchable. Women need to be kept out of the public sphere, and out of sacred spaces. They are damned by men for having bodies that allegedly inflame desire. But instead of controlling those men apparently thus inflamed, the law shuts women out of their Constitutional rights. Notwithstanding its ruling in 2018, then, the Supreme Court has quickly put its own judgment into abeyance and continues to condone rampant heterosexism.

IV: Homosexual

Like Section 497 on adultery, Section 377 IPC too is a colonial-era law that has a vexed relation to both naming and nature:

> Unnatural offences.—Whoever voluntarily has carnal intercourse against the order of nature with any man, woman or animal, shall be punished with imprisonment for life, or with imprisonment of either description for a term which may extend to ten years, and shall also be liable to fine.

This law describes its offence in the vaguest of terms: after all, what does 'carnal intercourse against the order of nature' mean? And (like the law against adultery) it criminalizes acts of consensual sex—'whoever *voluntarily* has carnal intercourse'. Casting a wide net, the law makes clear that the victims of carnal intercourse against the order of nature can be 'man, woman or animal'. However, the Section was popularly understood, by blackmailers and police alike, to refer primarily to homosexual men. It was to provide relief to this category of persons and to unsettle the equation of certain forms of carnality and criminality that the Supreme Court stepped in. In its welcome decision in *Navtej Johar vs Union of India* (2018) to read down Section 377 so as to exclude consensual sex between same-sex adults from the ambit of criminality, the Supreme Court finally endorsed the idea that consensual sex between adults must not be criminalized. Homosexual men and women were thus removed from the register of legal criminals.

But the Court did not quite address the question of what constitutes 'carnal acts against the order of nature' in the first place. In *Nimeshbhai Bharatbhai Desai vs State of Gujarat* (2018), the judge muses on the question of the natural and the unnatural. Quoting Black's Law Dictionary, Justice Pardiwala notes that in it, one of the definitions of the 'natural' is: '"The basic instincts or impulses of someone or something". To determine what is natural, functional basis is cited which basically means that every instrument or organ of the body has a particular function to perform, and therefore, using such an organ for a purpose inconsistent with its principal function is unnatural. As per this logic, every form of sex other than penile vaginal will be considered as unnatural. The same logic is used to denounce anything other than procreative sex as unnatural. This logic though prima facie illogical has been endorsed by the courts in various cases.'

'Natural' sex is considered to be hetero- and procreative sex; anything that does not fall within these functional parameters is legally deemed to be unnatural. Yet, were this definition to be enforced, then every sexually active person in the world would be a criminal since not every sexual interaction results in procreation. Lawyers' arguments in *Navtej Johar* missed a golden opportunity to emphasize human inter-connectedness in criminality. No matter what our sexual orientation, 377 potentially criminalized all of us for being 'unnatural'.

But the stakes of this case are even higher. If we are all potentially 'unnatural' in terms of having non-functional sex, then where does that leave the *idea* of unnatural sex acts? If homosexuality was legally unnatural until three years ago, and is legally natural today, then might that suggest there is something legally imprecise about the very category of the 'natural'? In addition to decriminalizing consensual same-sex relations, then, perhaps the Supreme Court needs to rethink the very use of 'natural' and 'unnatural' in relation to sex.

In many ways, what the *Navtej Johar* judgment has done is move rather than remove the legal boundary line separating natural from unnatural sex. It has naturalized many more people and sex acts while leaving intact the *category* of the unnatural to be occupied by other people and sex acts. This is why, for instance, Section 377 continues to criminalize human–animal sex. Whether or not we believe that bestiality should be decriminalized, the question posed by 377 is a different, and more important one: Do we take exception to any stigmatization of sex as unnatural, or do we simply not want *our* sex acts to be considered unnatural? When we ponder this question, we must remember that we are talking about a history in which the law has used the label of 'unnatural' to criminalize anything other than married, procreative sex. We are all, and all have been, legally unnatural, at one time or another.

Section 377 is just one instance of this legal unnaturalization of sex. In its pre-2018 iteration, 377 clubbed bestiality and homosexuality together as sexual crimes against the order of nature.[9] Now only bestiality is left to exemplify the burden of the unnatural. It is important to note that in order to stick to the category of the natural as a parameter for desire, there always has to be a category of the unnatural against which it can be compared. There will always have to be *some* sex act that is labelled unnatural. Yesterday it was homosexuality, today it is bestiality, tomorrow it might be threesomes. The question is thus not about whether or not we want to legalize human–animal sex. Rather, the question is whether we want to get rid of the idea of some sex being more natural than others. *Navtej Johar* ruled against the idea of gay sex being unnatural, but it has left intact the category of the unnatural to be mobilized in relation to sex.

One of the petitioners in the case makes this mobilization very clear. Arguing against lifting the stigma of criminality from same-sex sex acts, he asserts that 'it is well within the State's jurisdiction to put reasonable restrictions to forbid such *aberrant* human behaviour by means of legislation, for it is the duty of the State that people with *abnormal* conduct are prohibited from *imperilling* the life, health and security of the community. *Unrestrained pleasure*, and that too of a *lascivious* nature, is not conducive for the growth of a civilised society, such *inordinate gratification* needs to be *curbed*' (my emphasis). This vituperation against homosexual acts for being dangerous, obscene, and abnormal makes clear that the social fabric always needs a scapegoat (which might sometimes be an actual goat) onto which to project its anxieties about sex. And if that scapegoat is not us, then it will need to be somebody else. If not now, then soon.

On the basis of the legal definition of what counts as 'natural' sex, we are, every one of us, fugitives from the law. But certain categories take the fall for us all. The Cross-Religious Couple, The Transgendered Body, The Adulterous Wife, The Menstruating Woman, The Homosexual Man—these are the categories that have historically, legally, and socially, been termed unnatural.[10] We should therefore be wary of leaving the category of the 'unnatural' intact even as we celebrate the lifting of the stigma against gay sex. We should be aware that it is a category that will always need to be occupied, because the law always needs a desire against which to legislate. Exempting individual desires from the purview of the law does not lift the curtain of criminality from sex.

AMENDMENT

If the law does wrong by desire, then does the way ahead lie in rights?

In the wake of the *Navtej Johar* judgment in 2018, activists and lawyers have been agitating to legalize same-sex marriage. Their arguments hinge on two matters. First, that marriage is widely recognized in Indian society as the public face of private desire. And second, that marriage is the repository of rights, and therefore, should be made as available to homosexual people as to heterosexual people.[1]

Let us examine this case. There is no doubt that all citizens of a country should have equal rights. This is not a matter of dispute. What is more contentious, however, is whether marriage might be the best route by which to access those rights. Attaching certain rights exclusively to the institution of marriage not only ensures large-scale discrimination against those who are not married, but it also lays down the norm for what *kind* of desire is considered legitimate. As it currently stands, the rights attendant upon marriage are available only to the category of married monogamous heterosexual couples. Thus, those people who want to enter into the institution of marriage will have to abide by those same constraints on desire. While the 377 judgment does not say so explicitly, the wide use, in the lead-up to the judgment, of the sentimentalized language of 'love' to describe homosexual partnerships, makes this constraint all-too evident. The most powerful depiction of this language was on the cover of *India Today* in December 2013: a photo of Vikram Seth holding a slate on which is written—'Not a Criminal: To not be able to love the one you love is to have your life wrenched away, says Vikram Seth'. The 'one' that one 'loves' might now be a same-sex one, but it can still only be one and you have to make sure that you love it. While the configuration of love might have expanded from hetero- to homo-sexual, the conditions of recognition—monogamy and coupledom (in private)—remain firmly in place. Such an expansion of the empire of marriage thus disenfranchises sex workers, threesomes, and all those, including unmarried heterosexual people who, for various reasons, might not want to be in a monogamous relationship. The desire to be granted rights is always fulfilled at someone else's expense. Instead of asking the burning question of why any of our rights as citizens should depend on who we have sex with and how often, the rush to join Marriage Inc. seriously jeopardizes the argument for sexual and gendered freedom.

Indeed, from the anti-national marriage in Hadiya's case, to the rescue and rehabilitation marriage for devadasis and tawaifs, to the condemnation of women's extra-marital sexual pleasures as obscene, and the spectre of marriages being torn apart by adulterous wives, this book has repeatedly stumbled on marriage as a legal and moral *obstacle* to sexual desire. To think of marriage, then, as a badge of freedom and citizenship, is to ignore the violence perpetrated in the name of marriage against all sexual minorities. Since its inception, anyone not conforming to the model of the monogamous and reproductive heterosexual couple has been denuded of rights bestowed by the law. And even within the unit of such couples, women have continually been disenfranchised as the lesser partner. Is the answer to this disadvantage, then, to seek admission to the institution of marriage, or is it to chart a different course?[2] How can we get our rights and eat them too without attending a wedding feast?

There might be a way. Can we make a case for the law to practise non-discrimination: all citizens are granted the same rights of inheritance, medical visits, property ownership, tax exemptions, immigration, adoption, etc., that are currently premised on the condition of marriage?[3] These rights would be universal rather than specific. This means that instead of positing a particular category—heterosexuals, homosexuals—as the recipient of rights, the law would grant rights to everyone regardless of their desiring configurations. Like universal suffrage, which confers the right to vote on all people above the age of eighteen, regardless of whether they're old or lesbian or transmen, universal rights too would legally unhitch rights from marriage and remove the glitter that currently attaches to heterosexuality.[4]

But even the case for universal rights uncoupled from desire is not foolproof: it suffers from some of the same constraints that attend the idea of gay marriage by being discriminatory in nature. Granting rights to a defined category of people automatically excludes other categories that will not be given access to those same rights. This is a major problem with any attempt to reform the law because different reforms will be subject to a different set of constraints. Even if we legally uncouple rights from desires, then, we will have universal rights for most, but not all, desiring configurations. Which is to say, these rights will not be universal at all.

But if we turn back to a consideration of the marriage proposal, then another danger rears its head. The institution of marriage presumes that desire can be divided into neatly defined categories, all of which will compete with one another to receive Most Favoured Desire status under the law. But the dirty secret of the law is that *it* is the one that needs to categorize acts and identities and peoples. The law needs to distinguish between legality and illegality, especially in a terrain as vast and unpredictable as desire. It would thus be a mistake on our part to presume that these legal categories are synonymous with desire. If we follow the lead of the law, then we will be duped into believing that desire exists in categories rather than realizing that categories are what the law invents in order to make sense of desire. If we continue to fight for the inclusion of one *category* or another into the space of marriage, then, we will be speaking the language of the law rather than of desire. To speak the language of desire would entail not speaking in terms of categorical divisions but to realize that, potentially, all desire will always be suspect in the eyes of legalistic classification. Straddling the realms of religion and commerce and art and society, desire always overflows the confines of legal bounds.

We should insist, therefore, not on 'marriage for all', but rather on 'marriage for none'. We should be free to get married, of course, especially if we have a lot of money to spare. But marriage should not confer any special *legal* status on us. It should not be used as a legal hammer with which to nail the waywardness of desire. What happens when a same-sex partner dies intestate? How do we manage if a same-sex partner has not designated a partner as her primary care provider before slipping into a coma? What do we do if our child does not have both same-sex partners' names on its birth certificate? These are the legal issues that we need to work on and iron out.[5] But even as we do this, we should be clear that we cannot allow the law to mandate our sex lives or the horizon of our desires. We need to come up with non-marital mechanisms with which to designate our heirs, and sign property papers with co-owners of our choice, and assign our medical care to who we trust, regardless of with whom and how many people we might be having sex. Desire is not administrative. And marriage should not be given the honour of bestowing rights that the mere fact of citizenship should guarantee. We need to play with, rather than stay with, the Law of Desire.

ANNEXURE I

Notes

CRIMINAL

1 The Allahabad High Court has to date (January 2021) passed three orders against the separation of inter-religious couples and the subsequent imprisoning of the Muslim husband. It has stated repeatedly that adults have the Constitutional right to marry whom they want and profess whatever religion they will, and that the State has no right to interfere with those decisions. A public interest litigation challenging the UP Ordinance awaits hearing in the Supreme Court. Additionally, the Allahabad High Court has also said that the thirty-day public notice period that is demanded under the Special Marriage Act should be made optional rather than mandatory. This notice period is often used by vigilantes to police the women who marry men from other religions.

2 Even though inter-religious marriages in India inevitably take place under the Special Marriage Act, they do not always need to. Technically, Christians can marry non-Christians under Christian Law in India, and Muslim men can marry kitabias—people of the Book, i.e. Jews and Christians—under Sunni law. Muslim women, however, cannot marry non-Muslims under Sunni law.

3 In the cultural imagination, the most famous case associated with divorced Muslim women in the subcontinent is the *Mohd. Ahmed Khan vs Shah Bano Begum* in 1985.

The Supreme Court upheld the judgment of the Madhya Pradesh High Court that the husband has to pay monthly maintenance to his divorced wife if she is unable to maintain herself. This payment, they directed, has to be made even beyond the iddat period, which is three months after the divorce. Buckling to pressure from conservative quarters—some of whom took exception to Chief Justice Chandrachud's pejorative characterization of Muslims—the Rajiv Gandhi government in 1986 enacted the Muslim Women (Protection of Rights on Divorce) Act, which undid the Shah Bano judgment, and required Muslim men only to provide maintenance to divorced wives during the iddat period. However, a later judgment, in *Danial Latifi vs Union of India* in 2001, provided a creative workaround to the new law by ordering men to pay maintenance of an amount that will last for the lifetime of the divorced wife. The biggest difference from the Muslim Women (Protection of Rights on Marriage) Act is that Muslim men were not criminalized as they were later to be under the 2019 Act.

4 In fact, 'customary' divorce is prevalent also among Hindu communities. It is recognized under Section 29 of the 1955 Hindu Marriage Act, which states that: 'Nothing contained in this Act shall be deemed to affect any right recognised by custom or conferred by any special enactment to obtain the dissolution of a Hindu marriage, whether solemnised before or after the commencement of this Act.' If the marriage has been formally solemnized under recognized Hindu ritual, then customary divorce is not expected to apply. See, for instance, the 2019 judgment in *Banumathi vs The Regional Manager* (https://indiankanoon.org/doc/120884748/?type=print). In this case, as in others, customary divorce is only rendered illegal rather than

being judged criminal. We should also note, in this regard, Justice Indu Malhotra's judgment in the case that struck down the criminality of adultery, *Joseph Shine vs Union of India* in 2018: 'adultery is a marital wrong, which should have only civil consequences. A wrong punishable with criminal sanctions, must be a public wrong against society as a whole, and not merely an act committed against an individual victim'.

5 Overruling a 2015 judgment that said a 2005 amendment to the 1956 Hindu Succession Act would not have retrospective effect, a three-judge bench of the Supreme Court in August 2020 stated that daughters born before 2005 too would be considered equal coparceners in relation to undivided ancestral property. However, even as Hindu women had to wait till 2020 to get these inheritance rights, the judgment assured male Hindus that their inheritance rights would not be affected (how is this possible when the pie is allegedly being carved now into smaller pieces?), and that all ancestral property that had already been divided before 2004 among the sons could not now be claimed by daughters. It is also worth remembering that, legally, even now, the unit of the Hindu joint family can only be headed by a man.

IMMORAL

1 The newest Bill to govern all forms of trafficking, and passed by the Lok Sabha in 2018, drops the word 'prostitute' altogether from its lexicon. Styling itself as The Trafficking of Persons (Prevention, Protection and Rehabilitation) Bill, the twenty-four-page Bill uses the word 'victim' 88 times. The fact that it was introduced in the Lok Sabha by the Minister of Women and Child Development, Maneka

Gandhi, suggests the link between trafficking and women. And when the Bill's definition states that trafficking 'includes physical or sexual exploitation', then the link between trafficking and prostitution becomes clear.

2 The terminology of 'prostitute' maps quite nicely onto 'veshya' and 'ganika' and 'tawaif' from the Indian lexicon. But none of these words contain the moral opprobrium with which the English language has invested 'prostitution'. In some ways, I am trying to reclaim the word 'prostitute' by separating it from a register of immorality. To this end, the Latin etymology of 'prostitute' is useful—deriving as it does from the Latin 'pro' (before, in front of), and 'statutere' (place; location). It etymologically refers to placing something openly, which has then been expanded to understand goods offered publicly for sale.

3 Indeed, the status of trafficked victim is potentially changed to that of volitional professional when sex emerges out of the private and into the public sphere. Even though there are thousands of victims of sex trafficking who are indeed in need of rescuing, the framework of rescue and rehabilitation is the *only* one the law can envisage in relation to commercial sex.

4 'Freedom' and 'identity' seem to have become the flag-bearers for stamping out sex work: the common socio-legal assumption is that women are imprisoned within sex work and need to be freed from it. This freedom will then lead to their occupying their 'true' identity as good (rather than 'fallen') women. Svati B. Shah traces this intricate ontological web of sexual identities and freedoms: 'Cases regarding lesbian, gay, queer, and transgender rights issues have been largely successful by codifying all sexuality as fixed, thus allowing for an ethnicized, and minoritized social status that can claim the right to recognition and

protection by the state. This is part of a strategic trend towards using the rhetoric of biology to argue for gay rights... The overall trend...therefore, is towards presenting homosexuality, gayness, and the like as unchanging identity constructs, as an aspect of the authentic, ontological truth of an individual... [But] if homosexuality is the authentic truth of an individual, articulated through having consensual, decriminalized sex in private, then selling sex is rendered a lie, because monetizing the sex act alienates sex from love, the other aspect of sex in private that underlies this rationale for the need to decriminalize sodomy... [T]his strategy has run the risk of further stigmatizing sex as labour as being somehow "inauthentic"' (Shah, 'True Sex and the Law', pp. 171–2).

5 In *Indian Sex Life: Sexuality and the Colonial Origins of Modern Social Thought*, Durba Mitra points out that: 'In 1872, the British colonial state initiated its most ambitious and extensive knowledge-gathering survey about Indian women. The inquiry was spurred by a new law against the buying and selling of girls for the purpose of prostitution, passed under the 1860 Indian Penal Code—perhaps the first law against trafficking anywhere in the world. In this widely distributed questionnaire, the Government of India asked a deceptively simple question: Who was a prostitute in India?... In the responses, local colonial administrators answered that *all* Indian women were potential prostitutes' (p. 62).

6 Several individual judgments have recommended criminalizing marital rape. Perhaps the most emphatic statements have been made in *Nimeshbhai Bharatbhai Desai vs State of Gujarat*. In its 2018 judgment, the Court states that '[m]arital rape is a disgraceful offence that has scarred the trust and confidence in the institution of

marriage. A large population of women has faced the brunt of the non-criminalization of the practice'.

7 The existence of such laws has since spread to three other states—Karnataka, Andhra Pradesh, and Maharashtra, with the most recent legislation being The Maharashtra Devdasi System (Abolition) Act of 2005.

8 According to Rohit De, the birth of SITA too was presided over by women like Muthulakshmi Reddy, who very much had notions of sexual purity in mind in their opposition to prostitution. Durgabai Deshmukh, for instance, designated Planning Commission funds to conduct a nationwide survey on 'social and moral hygiene that became the basis for SITA. This survey was carried out by the Association for Social and Moral Hygiene (ASMH), a leading abolitionist organization in London...that achieved some success, beginning in 1928, in closing down military and public brothels' (De, *A People's Constitution*, p. 177).

9 Davesh Soneji brilliantly recounts this tendency of the left-wing to sound puritanical: 'Gandhi's reactions to devadāsīs are remarkably consistent: he felt repulsed by dāsīs and also used the familiar trope of false consciousness when it came to devadāsī resistance to reform. He refused to listen to devadāsī voices: "The opinion of the parties concerned in the immoral traffic cannot count, just as the opinion of keepers of opium dens will not count in favour of their retention, if public opinion is otherwise against them."' (Soneji, *Unfinished Gestures*, p. 133)

10 Durba Mitra quotes 'the deputy commissioner of the Police in Calcutta, A.H. Giles, who argued that all women outside of high-caste monogamous marriage could be classified as one of five types of prostitutes... "The prostitute community is recruited in various ways from all classes and castes. The greatest number of prostitutes are

perhaps Hindoo widows who have been seduced in their native village, and being out-casted have come to Calcutta to practice as prostitutes..."' (Mitra, *Indian Sex Life*, p. 62), and so on. She adds that in 'the new legal sociology of Indian sexual practices, women outside of monogamous marriage or who appeared in public spaces, participated in the labor force, and practiced kinship forms seen as backward and sexually promiscuous were equivalent to prostitutes' (ibid., p. 98).

11 Kunal M. Parker notes that 'As applied by Anglo-Indian courts, the Hindu law conditioned women's property rights upon their chastity. Although this position would dissolve during the second half of the nineteenth century, during the first half of the nineteenth century, women who violated the rigid controls on their sexual behaviour by engaging in what was variously, but vaguely, described as "prostitution", "unchastity" or "incontinence" suffered a degradation from caste by reason of which they forfeited their property'.

12 In *A People's Constitution*, Rohit De notes that 'According to the Allahabad High Court [in a verdict delivered in 1927], a public prostitute was a "woman who usually and generally offers her person to sexual intercourse for hire and who openly advertises and acknowledges her occupation by word of mouth, deportment, or conduct"... For a woman to escape regulations targeting public prostitutes, she would have to demonstrate that she was sexually exclusive or attached to a single man as a mistress... The courts privileged a certain kind of sexual commerce over others, reflecting a need to prevent the urban government from interfering with the sexual lives of upper-class men, who were the patrons of the more exclusive prostitutes' (p. 188).

OBSCENE

1 There are several 'tests' that the law has set over the years in order to aid its judgments on obscenity. The most notorious of these is the Hicklin Test, established by the British case of *Regina vs Hicklin* in 1868. The court there held that all material tending 'to deprave and corrupt those whose minds are open to such immoral influences' was obscene, regardless of artistic or literary merit. The Hicklin Test allows for portions of a work to be judged independent of context. If any portion may be deemed obscene, then the entire work can be outlawed; if any particularly susceptible person is shown to have been adversely affected by it, then the book or work of art can be termed obscene. The Roth Test, otherwise known as the 'community standards' test, and derived from the 1957 US Supreme Court judgment in *Roth vs United States*, states that obscenity depends on 'whether to the average person, applying contemporary community standards, the dominant theme of the material taken as a whole appeals to prurient interest'. The move from a susceptible person to an average person, and the shift from a portion of a text taken in isolation to a text taken in its entirety and in context, has marked an improvement in several legal judgments. However, the spectre of arbitrariness continues to cast its shadow over these and other 'tests'.

2 An instructive example in this regard is the 1942 trial in the Lahore High Court of Manto's close friend and associate, Ismat Chughtai, for her short story, 'Lihaaf'. Prosecuted for obscenity, Chughtai refused to apologize for the short story, and also went on to win the trial. Every witness for the prosecution was asked by Chughtai's lawyer to point to a single obscene word in the story with which to back

up their accusation. Every witness failed to do so. How, then, the lawyer demanded, can the story be obscene when there isn't a single obscene word in it? 'Lihaaf', widely considered to be one of the earliest lesbian stories from the Indian subcontinent, escaped being criminalized as obscene. Instead, it exemplified Manto's description of the potential obscenity of even the most banal words.

3 The English word 'obscene' refers, via Greek and Latin, to something not deemed fit to be seen, something that needs to be separated out from the official version of an event, contained and confined offstage.

4 Justice Sikri's judgment in 2018 is instructive in this regard. It overturned the Bombay Police ban on bar dancers because it was location-specific. The ban was only on lower-class establishments, while dancing in theatres, cinema halls, upper-class hotels and gymkhanas, was permitted. Justice Sikri found that such class discrimination violated Article 14 of the Constitution, which prohibits discrimination on the basis of sex, race, caste, creed and place of birth. In this regard, his judgment went directly against Justice Choudary's, ruling in favour of non-discrimination rather than actively supporting class discrimination. However, the 2018 judgment does not take issue with the idea that dances can be obscene and should be banned if found to be obscene; indeed, Justice Sikri states clearly that he has 'no quarrel' with banning dances in accordance with Section 294 of the IPC if they are obscene. And so, despite not using the same language as Justice Choudary's, this judgment too leaves the door open for class consciousness to return to verdicts about public dance performances. After all, upper and lower class map all too easily onto acceptable 'classical' and obscene 'popular' dance.

5 Indeed, Section 294 IPC itself defines 'obscene dance' as a

dance that 'is designed only to arouse the prurient interest of the audience'. The letter of the law criminalizes sex that is physically sexy and cannot be assimilated into the register of intellectual good.

6 As Gautam Bhatia notes of the judgment in *Aveek Sarkar vs State of West Bengal* (2014): 'in essence, it seems to be saying that if (on applying community standards), a particular work "*has a tendency to arouse feeling or reveal an overt sexual desire*", it can be criminalized as obscene. This is worse than vague. On what ground does the Court hold sexual arousal to be something that ought to be criminalized?'

7 In *Navtej Singh Johar & Ors vs Union of India* (2018), one of the intervenors made the following argument against the decriminalization of same-sex relations in private between consenting adults: 'it is well within the State's jurisdiction to put reasonable restrictions to forbid such aberrant human behaviour by means of legislation, for it is the duty of the State that people with abnormal conduct are prohibited from imperilling the life, health and security of the community. *Unrestrained pleasure, and that too of a lascivious nature, is not conducive for the growth of a civilised society*, such inordinate gratification needs to be curbed and, thus, prohibition against carnal intercourse as defined in Section 377 IPC does not violate the constitutional rights of a person' (my emphasis). The difference between 'pleasure' and its 'unrestrained' variety remains murky. In using this language, the intervenor echoes the unclear and uneasy relation between the obscenity laws and sex.

8 In his 1979 Delhi High Court judgment in *Raj Kapoor vs State*, for instance, Justice Krishna Iyer states explicitly that the voluptuous sculptures of naked bodies on temples like Konark and Khajuraho are not obscene.

UNNATURAL

1 Justice Sikri's concurring judgment in *NALSA*, while overwhelmingly positive, is marked by a lingering sense of transgenderism as an anomaly: 'It may also happen that though a person is born as a male, *because of some genital anatomy problems* his innate perception may be that of a female and all his actions would be female oriented. The position may be exactly the opposite wherein a person born as female may behave like a male person' (my emphasis).

2 Section 497 IPC states: Whoever has sexual intercourse with a person who is and whom he knows or has reason to believe to be the wife of another man, without the consent or connivance of that man, such sexual intercourse not amounting to the offence of rape, is guilty of the offence of adultery, and shall be punished with imprisonment of either description for a term which may extend to five years, or with fine, or with both. In such case the wife shall not be punishable as an abettor.

3 In her analysis of rape law and the 'exception' legally provided for marital rape, Avanija Inuganti notes that 'cases brought under Section 9 of the Hindu Marriage Act...[reveal] the patriarchal attitude of the judges while adjudicating upon the status of the "holy institution of marriage". Section 9 of HMA states that "when either the husband or the wife withdraws from the society without a reasonable excuse, the aggrieved party may file a petition for restitution of conjugal rights". Justice Choudhary [in *T. Sareeta vs Venkatasubbiah*, AIR 1983 AP 356] held that Section 9 of HMA is unconstitutional and opined that this provision can be used by the man to impose himself on his wife, without her consent or to molest or sexually abuse

her. This case was overruled by the Supreme Court and the constitutionality of Section 9 was upheld [*Saroj Rani vs Sudarshan Kumar*, AIR 1984 SC 1562]. The judge, in this case, stated that "conjugal rights are not merely a creation of the statute but is instead inherent in the institution of marriage itself". He also opined that Section 9 '"serves a social purpose as an aid to the prevention of break-up of marriage". This "need to preserve the sanctity of marriage" that is prevalent among the judges will act as a dangerous impediment to any sort of relief that the wife who files a rape case against her husband is seeking for, which makes the marital rape charge completely redundant.'

4 In his concurring judgment in *Joseph Shine*, Justice Chandrachud notes that: 'In restricting the sexual agency of women, Section 497 gives legal recognition to socially discriminatory and gender-based norms. Sexual relations for a woman were legally and socially permissible when it was within her marriage. Women who committed adultery or non-marital sex were labelled immoral, shameful, and were criminally condemned.'

5 Here is how the Supreme Court judgment itself introduces the case: 'Appellant Nanavati, a Naval Officer, was put up on trial under ss. 302 and 304 Part I of the Indian Penal Code for the alleged murder of his wife's paramour. The prosecution case in substance was that on the day of occurrence his wife Sylvia confessed to him of her illicit intimacy with Ahuja and the accused went to his ship, took from its stores a revolver and cartridges on a false pretext, loaded the same, went to Ahuja's flat, entered his bed room and shot him dead. The defence, inter alia, was that as his wife did not tell him if Ahuja would marry her and take charge of their children, he decided to go and settle the matter with him. He drove his wife and children to a

cinema where he dropped them promising to pick them up when the show ended at 6 p.m., drove to the ship and took the revolver and the cartridges on a false pretext intending to shoot himself. Then he drove his car to Ahuja's office and not finding him there, drove to his flat. After an altercation a struggle ensued between the two and in course of that struggle two shots went off accidentally and hit Ahuja. Evidence, oral and documentary, was adduced in the case including three letters written by Sylvia to Ahuja. Evidence was also given of an extra-judicial confession made by the accused to prosecution witness 12 who deposed that the accused when leaving the place of occurrence told him that he had a quarrel with Ahuja as the latter had "connections" with his wife and therefore he killed him. This witness also deposed that he told P.W. 13, Duty Officer at the Police Station, what the accused had told him. This statement was not recorded by P.W. 13 and was denied by him in his cross-examination. In his statement to the investigation officer it was also not recorded. The jury returned a verdict of "not guilty" on both the charges by a majority of 8:1. The Sessions Judge disagreed with that verdict, as in his view, no reasonable body of men could bring that verdict on the evidence and referred the matter to the High Court under s. 307 of the Code of Criminal Procedure. The two Judges of the Division Bench who heard the matter agreed in holding that the appellant was guilty under s. 302 of the Indian Penal Code and sentenced him to undergo rigorous imprisonment for life... On appeal to this Court by special leave it was contended on behalf of the appellant that... there were no misdirections in the charge [to the jury] nor was the verdict perverse and that since there was grave and sudden provocation the offence committed if any, was not murder but culpable homicide not amounting to murder.' The appeal was denied by the Supreme Court, and Nanavati was sent to prison. The Bombay Governor later stepped in with a pardon, Nanavati was freed, and the family emigrated to Toronto, where Kawas Nanavati died in 2003, and where Sylvia Nanavati still lives.

6 Women's bodies and desires seem so frightening to the law that they do not want to interfere with 'custom'. Of course, this non-interference policy tends to happen only in relation to the so-called customs of the majority religion. One of the questions before the Court was whether Ayyappan devotees are Hindus or not. Four of the five judges said Ayyappans are 'Hindus' and therefore the State is allowed to bring their practices in line with constitutional morality. But Justice Indu Malhotra demurred. Here is a summary of the dissenting judgment's view on this question: 'She held that the Sabarimala Temple satisfies the requirements for being considered a separate religious denomination. She therefore held that the Sabarimala Temple is protected under Article 26 (b) to manage its internal affairs and is not subject to the social reform mandate under Article 25 (2) (b), which applies only to Hindu denominations. Note that Article 26, denominational freedom of religion, is subject to "*public order, morality and health*". Justice Malhotra held that "morality" (constitutional morality) must be understood in the context of India being a pluralistic society. She stated that the State must respect the freedom of various individuals and sects to practice their faith.

'She held that the fundamental right to equality guaranteed to women under Article 14 cannot override Article 25, which guarantees every individual the right to profess, practice and propagate their faith.' (See https://www.scobserver.in/court-case/sabrimala-temple-entry-case/plain-english-summary-of-judgment-ee5ae148-9597-479f-84d7-35d398ed5e68)

7 As he often does, Justice Chandrachud nails this argument on its head: 'The Respondents submitted that the deity at Sabarimala is in the form of a Naishtika Brahmacharya: Lord Ayyappa is celibate. It was submitted that since celibacy is the foremost requirement for all the followers, women between the ages of ten and fifty must not be allowed in Sabarimala. There is an assumption here, which cannot stand constitutional scrutiny. The assumption in such a claim is that a deviation from the celibacy and austerity observed by the followers would be caused by the presence of women. Such a claim cannot be sustained as a constitutionally sustainable argument. Its effect is to impose the burden of a man's celibacy on a woman and construct her as a cause for deviation from celibacy. This is then employed to deny access to spaces to which women are equally entitled. To suggest that women cannot keep the Vratham is to stigmatise them and stereotype them as being weak and lesser human beings.' However, this understanding of the unnamed burden on women's sexuality did not feature in Justice Chandrachud's thinking in *Joseph Shine*.

8 In keeping with the political zeitgeist, the expansion of the Sabarimala case's ambit to a consideration of the practices of 'other religions' seems to be an attempt to shield the noxious practices of patriarchal Hinduism from scrutiny while simultaneously vilifying minority religions. The Court balks at asking Hindus to change their rules, while it has felt perfectly free to interfere with the customs of minority communities in order to 'free' their women from oppressive practices—the Triple Talaq verdict being a case in point. As the pushback against the Sabarimala

judgment makes clear, the desire for a Uniform Civil Code will receive the maximum resistance from Hindus.

9 Bestiality is legal in several parts of the world—Congo, Madagascar, Angola, Mozambique, partially in Jamaica, Chile, Japan, Cambodia, Hungary, Romania, Belarus, Finland, and Albania, among others. These and other countries have separate laws dealing with cruelty to animals that provide sufficient protection to animals against torture.

10 Historically, it is men rather than women who have faced religiously- and socially-sanctioned ire against homosexuality. The Book of Leviticus in the Bible, the Quran, and other religious texts mention only male homosexuality (although Leviticus does mention female bestiality). Part of this owes to a lack of imagination—the men who wrote these texts couldn't imagine women being sexually interested in anyone other than men (although by that token, it is interesting that they were able to imagine men interested in other men!). Part of this owes to a lack of power—women are so disempowered by heterosexuality that their desires are simply not taken seriously enough. And part of this might owe to the fact that men protect heterosexuality more zealously than women might (perhaps because it doesn't have much to offer us?). Despite all these reasons, though, there has been and continues to be horrific homophobia directed against women who have sex with women, even as historically, these desires have never been the subjects of either religious or secular laws.

AMENDMENT

1 Ratna Kapur has warned against sexual minorities relying overly on a rights discourse to gain advantages that have historically been denied them. Arvind Narrain and Alok Gupta have cautioned against the blunting of opposition to legal violence if we all clamour to be admitted to the same oppressive State institutions. And Upendra Baxi has pointed out that a blanket human rights discourse might constitute 'a vast conceptual and criteriological prison house' in which everyone is trapped within their identities as recognized by the law, and no movement is allowed beyond these identities.

2 Kunal M. Parker points out the historical obsession with marriage, especially among Hindu communities: 'As expounded by Strange, the Hindu law's pronouncements with respect to women revealed an obsession with marriage. Virtually all legal rights, duties, incapacities and disabilities in respect of women were constructed around marriage. The broad principle of marriage as a "sacrament" ordained for women cannot have been distasteful to early colonial commentators.'

3 Suhrith Parthasarathy notes that 'India is unique among democracies in that a constitutional right to equality is not backed by comprehensive legislation'.

4 As the next paragraph makes clear, there is really no such thing as universal suffrage. In India, you can be disqualified from voting if you are convicted under Sections 125, 135, and 136 IPC, all of which deal with military matters and national security. Or if you have committed an offence under 171E and F of the IPC, both of which deal with bribery and electoral impersonation.

5 In current legal conditions, if a married person dies

intestate, then their property would automatically (after a lot of bureaucratic paperwork) accrue to their married spouse, or to the parents/children in the absence of a spouse. Legal provisions to nominate one's heir are available to all citizens. But in the absence of marriage and in the absence of legal nominations, unmarried partners are legally at a considerable disadvantage. How do we 'prove' next-of-kin status without reverting to ties of blood? How do we recognize affective bonds as being legally viable? How do we recognize unmarried sex as being affectively tenable? These are the logistical questions with which we need to grapple.

ANNEXURE II

Bibliography

'Adultery in India: Law, Court and Sanctity of Marriage'. *RGICS Policy Watch*, vol. 7, no. 5, October 11, 2018, pp. 1–12.

'Conversion Therapy for Homosexuality: Serious Violation of Ethics'. *Indian Journal of Medical Ethics*, July 4, 2016 (ijme.in/articles/conversion-therapy-for-homosexuality-serious-violation-of-ethics/?galley=html, last accessed October 19, 2021).

'Countries and Their Prostitution Policies'. *ProCon.org* (https://prostitution.procon.org/countries-and-their-prostitution-policies/, last accessed October 19, 2021).

'Decriminalise Sex Work: CGE'. *ENCA*, May 16, 2013 (https://www.enca.com/south-africa/decriminalise-sex-work-cge, last accessed October 19, 2021).

'Gay rights protests across India against Supreme Court ruling on homosexuality'. *NDTV*, December 15, 2013 (https://www.ndtv.com/india-news/gay-rights-protests-across-india-against-supreme-court-ruling-on-homosexuality-544615, last accessed October 19, 2021).

'Important International Jurisprudence Concerning LGBT Rights'. *Human Rights Watch*, July 29, 2020 (https://www.hrw.org/news/2009/05/25/important-international-jurisprudence-concerning-lgbt-rights, last accessed October 19, 2021).

'Karachi fast becoming a hub of male prostitution'. *DNA India*, April 27, 2010 (https://www.dnaindia.com/world/

report-karachi-fast-becoming-a-hub-of-male-prostitution-1376236, last accessed October 19, 2021).

'Pandering, Prostitution and Disorderly Houses'. Nevada Revised Statute Chapter 201: Crimes Against Public Decency and Good Morals (available online: www.leg.state.nv.us/NRS/NRS-201.html, last accessed October 19, 2021).

'Prostitution in the United States'. *HG.org* (https://www.hg.org/legal-articles/prostitution-in-the-united-states-30997, last accessed October 19, 2021).

'Prostitution Reform Act 2003, No. 28 (Reprint as at 26 November 2018)'. New Zealand Legislation, official website of the New Zealand Parliamentary Counsel Office (available online: https://www.legislation.govt.nz/act/public/2003/0028/latest/DLM197815.html).

'Sex Work in Asia'. World Health Organization, Regional Office for the Western Pacific, July 2001 (available online: https://web.archive.org/web/20080920224846/http://www.wpro.who.int/NR/rdonlyres/D01A4265-A142-4E19-99AE-6CC7E44F995C/0/Sex_Work_in_Asia_July2001.pdf, last accessed October 19, 2021).

'Sexual Offences Act 2003'. *Legislation.gov.uk*, Statute Law Database (https://www.legislation.gov.uk/ukpga/2003/42/part/1/crossheading/exploitation-of-prostitution).

'Sexual Offences Act, 1956'. Act of the Parliament of the United Kingdom (available online: http://www.legislation.gov.uk/ukpga/1956/69/pdfs/ukpga_19560069_en.pdf, last accessed October 19, 2021).

'US Supreme Court backs Colorado baker's gay wedding cake snub'. *BBC News*, June 4, 2018 (https://www.bbc.com/news/world-us-canada-44361162, last accessed October 19, 2021).

Admin. 'A Legal Guide to Prostitution'. *Laws.com* (https://sex-crimes.laws.com/prostitution/prostitution, last accessed October 19, 2021).

Agnes, Flavia. *Law and Gender Inequality: The Politics of Women's Rights in India*. Oxford University Press, 2001.

———. 'Reforms as If Women Mattered'. *Manushi*, no. 119 (available online: http://www.indiatogether.org/manushi/issue119/reforms.htm, last accessed October 19, 2021).

———. 'Justice for Hadiya'. Author's blog (https://flaviaagnes.wordpress.com/2017/09/07/justice-for-hadiya/, last accessed October 19, 2021).

Ali, Sabir. '"The Public and the Private: Issues of Democratic Citizenship."' *Social Change*, 2003.

Balasubrahmanyan, Vimal. 'Gay Rights in India'. *Economic and Political Weekly*, vol. 31, no. 5, February 3, 1996, pp. 257–58 (https://www.jstor.org/stable/4403740).

Bapat, Jyotsna. 'Experiencing Love as Devadasi Tradition'. *Academia* (https://www.academia.edu/19680979/Experiencing_Love_as_Devadasi_Tradition, last accessed October 19, 2021).

Barnett, Laura, and Lyne Casavant. 'Prostitution: A Review of Legislation in Selected Countries'. Library of Parliament, Ottawa, Canada, Background Paper no. 2011-115-E, November 3, 2011.

Basu, Srimati. *She Comes to Take Her Rights: Indian Women, Property, and Propriety*. Kali for Women, 2001.

Baxi, Upendra. *Towards a Sociology of Indian Law*. Satvahan, 1986.

———. *The Future of Human Rights*. Oxford University Press, 2012.

Bhatia, Gautam. *The Transformative Constitution: A Radical Biography in Nine Acts*. Harper Collins India, 2019.

Bhattacharji, Sukumari. 'Prostitution in Ancient India'. *Social Scientist*, vol. 15, no. 2, February 1987, pp. 32–61 (http://www.jstor.org/stable/3520437).

Bhattacharya, Neeladri. '"Remaking Custom: The Discourse and Practice of Colonial Codification."' In *Tradition, Dissent and Ideology: Essays in Honour of Romila Thapar*, edited by R. Champakalakshmi and S. Gopal, Oxford University Press, 1996, pp. 20–51.

Bureau, Outlook Web. 'How Husbands Accused Wives Of Adultery: Five Cases From The Past'. *Outlook*, September 26, 2018 (https://www.outlookindia.com/website/story/how-husbands-accused-wives-of-adultery-five-cases-from-the-past/317276, last accessed October 19, 2021).

Butalia, Urvashi. 'Abducted and Widowed Women: Questions of Sexuality and Citizenship During Partition'. In *Embodiment: Essays on Gender and Identity*, edited by Meenakshi Thapan, Oxford University Press, 1997, pp. 91–106 (available online: http://jan.ucc.nau.edu/~sj6/butaliaabductedwomen.pdf, last accessed October 19, 2021).

Casciani, Dominic. 'Q&A: UK Prostitution Laws'. *BBC News*, November 19, 2008 (news.bbc.co.uk/2/hi/uk_news/7736436.stm, last accessed October 19, 2021).

Chandrachud, Abhinav. *Republic of Religion: The Rise and Fall of Colonial Secularism in India*. Penguin/Viking, 2020.

Chatterjee, Partha. 'Colonialism, Nationalism, and Colonialized Women: The Contest in India'. *American Ethnologist*, vol. 16, no. 4, November 1989, pp. 622–33.

Chattopadhyaya, Partha. *State and Politics in India*. Oxford University Press, 1997.

Choudhry, Sujit, Madhav Khosla, and Pratap Bhanu Mehta. *The Oxford Handbook of the Indian Constitution*. Oxford University Press, 2016.

Cohn, Bernard S. *Colonialism and its Forms of Knowledge: The British in India.* Princeton University Press, 2006.

Contractor, Qudsiya. 'Muslim Women and the Challenge of Religion in Contemporary Mumbai'. *Economic and Political Weekly*, vol. 52, no. 42–43, October 28, 2017.

———, Sumita Menon, and Ravi Duggal, ed. *Sex Selection Issues & Concerns: A Compilation of Writings.* Centre for Enquiry into Health and Allied Themes Survey, 2003.

Cossman, Brenda, and Ratna Kapur. *Secularism's Last Sigh?: Hindutva and the (Mis)Rule of Law.* Oxford University Press, 2001.

Dalwai, Sameena. 'Caste and the Bar Dancer'. *Economic and Political Weekly*, vol. 48, no. 48, November 30, 2013.

Das, Veena. *Life and Words: Violence and the Descent into the Ordinary.* University of California Press, 2006.

De, Rohit. 'Mumtaz Bibi's Broken Heart: The Many Lives of the Dissolution of Muslim Marriages Act'. *Indian Economic and Social History Review*, vol. 46, no. 1, 2009, pp. 105–30 (https://doi.org/10.1177/001946460804600106).

———. *A People's Constitution: The Everyday Life of Law in the Indian Republic.* Princeton University Press, 2018.

Deady, Gail M. 'The Girl Next Door: A Comparative Approach to Prostitution Laws and Sex Trafficking Victim Identification Within the Prostitution Industry'. *Washington and Lee Journal of Civil Rights and Social Justice*, vol. 17, no. 2, April 1, 2011, pp. 516–55 (https://scholarlycommons.law.wlu.edu/crsj/vol17/iss2/7).

Devasia, T.K. 'Kerala "love jihad" case fallout: Hadiya's father has transformed from staunch atheist to hardcore Hindutvavadi'. *Firstpost*, Dcember 18, 2018 (https://www.firstpost.com/india/kerala-love-jihad-case-fallout-hadiyas-father-has-transformed-from-staunch-atheist-to-hardcore-hindutvavadi-5751371.html, last accessed October 19, 2021).

Dhavan, Rajeev. 'Codifying Personal Law'. *The Hindu*, August 1, 2003.

Dube, Siddharth. 'Minding Their Business: The Unfinished Battle for Sex Workers' Rights'. *The Caravan*, June 1, 2020 (https://caravanmagazine.in/reportage/unfinished-battle-sex-workers-rights, last accessed October 19, 2021).

FP Staff. 'Full text of the judgment: Supreme Court strikes down Section 497 of IPC, rules adultery law as unconstitutional'. *Firstpost*, September 27, 2018 (https://www.firstpost.com/india/full-text-of-the-judgment-supreme-court-strikes-down-section-497-rules-adultery-law-as-unconstitutional-5274431.html, last accessed October 19, 2021).

Gavison, Ruth. 'Feminism and the Public/Private Distinction'. *Stanford Law Review*, vol. 45, no. 1, 1992, p. 1 (https://doi.org/10.2307/1228984).

Gupta, Charu. *Sexuality, Obscenity, Community: Women, Muslims, and the Hindu Public in Colonial India*. Permanent Black, 2001.

Jaising, Indira. 'The Ghost of Narasu Appa Mali is stalking the Supreme Court of India'. *The Leaflet*, May 28, 2018 (https://www.theleaflet.in/specialissues/the-ghost-of-narasu-appa-mali-is-stalking-the-supreme-court-of-india-by-indira-jaising/, last accessed October 19, 2021).

Kapur, Ratna. *Erotic Justice: Law and the New Politics of Postcolonialism*. Routledge-Cavendish, 2016.

_____. *Gender, Alterity and Human Rights: Freedom in a Fishbowl*. Edward Elgar, 2020.

_____. 'Sexcapades and the Law'. *Seminar*, no. 505, September 2001, pp. 40-53.

———, and Brenda Cossman. 'On Women, Equality and the Constitution: Through the Looking Glass of Feminism'. *Feminism and Law*, special issue of the *National Law School Journal*, no. 1, 1993, pp. 1–61.

Karkaria, Bachi. 'Sylvia's story beyond the scandal'. *Livemint*, May 2, 2017 (https://www.livemint.com/Leisure/OGsgT6hkkniURonylB2uXK/Sylvias-story-beyond-the-scandal.html, last accessed October 19, 2021).

———. *In Hot Blood: The Nanavati Case that Shook India*. Juggernaut, 2017.

Kirpal, B.H., and H. Desai. *Supreme But Not Infallible: Essays in Honour of the Supreme Court of India*. Oxford University Press, 2000.

Kirpal, Saurabh. *Sex and the Supreme Court: How the Law is Upholding the Dignity of the Indian Citizen*. Hachette, 2020.

———. 'Why It's Time to Consider Same Sex Marriage'. *Article 14: Justice. Constitution. Democracy* (website), October 21, 2020 (https://www.article-14.com/post/why-it-s-time-to-consider-same-sex-marriage, last accessed October 19, 2021).

Koppel, Nathan. 'Louisiana's "Crime Against Nature" Sex Law Draws Legal Fire'. *The Wall Street Journal*, February 16, 2011 (https://www.wsj.com/articles/BL-LB-39292, last accessed October 19, 2021).

Koshi, Nikita. 'Explained: Will ruling against Caster Semenya see intersex athletes switching events'. *Indian Express*, September 13, 2020 (https://indianexpress.com/article/explained/cas-ruling-on-caster-semenyas-appeal-6590024/, last accessed October 19, 2021).

Kotamraju, Priyanka, and Sibi Arasu. 'Gay activist groups erupt in protest over apex court verdict on Section

377'. *The Hindu BusinessLine*, March 12, 2018 (https://www.thehindubusinessline.com/news/gay-activist-groups-erupt-in-protest-over-apex-court-verdict-on-section-377/article20698213.ece1, last accessed October 19, 2021).

Kotiswaran, Prabha. 'How Did We Get Here? Or A Short History of the 2018 Trafficking Bill'. *Economic and Political Weekly*, vol. 53, no. 29, July 20, 2018.

Kumar Dash, Dipak, and Sanjay Yadav. 'In a first, Gurgaon court recognizes lesbian marriage'. *The Times of India*, July 29, 2011 (https://timesofindia.indiatimes.com/city/gurgaon/In-a-first-Gurgaon-court-recognizes-lesbian-marriage/articleshow/9401421.cms, last accessed October 19, 2021).

Lingat, Robert. *The Classical Law of India*. Translated by J. Duncan M. Derret. Rev. ed., Oxford University Press, India, 1998.

Macnaghten, Sir W.H. *Principles and Precedents of Moohummudan Law*. 2nd ed., Atheneum Press, 1860.

Mahajan, Shruti. '"It will leave society in a very bad taste", Supreme Court dismisses anticipatory bail plea by activist Rehana Fathima', *Bar and Bench*, August 7, 2020 (https://www.barandbench.com/news/litigation/it-will-leave-society-in-a-very-bad-taste-supreme-court-dismisses-anticipatory-bail-plea-by-activist-rehana-fathima, last accessed October 19, 2021).

Mani, Lata. *Contentious Traditions: The Debate on Sati in Colonial India*. University of California Press, 1998.

McCarthy, Julie. 'Indian Supreme Court Declares Privacy A Fundamental Right'. *NPR*, August 24, 2017 (https://www.npr.org/sections/thetwo-way/2017/08/24/545963181/indian-supreme-court-declares-privacy-a-fundamental-right, last accessed October 19, 2021).

McClintock, Anne. 'Screwing the System: Sexwork, Race, and the Law'. *Boundary 2*, vol. 19, no. 2, 1992, pp. 70–95 (https://doi.org/10.2307/303534).

McKay, Carolyn. 'Murder Ob/Scene: The Seen, Unseen and Ob/scene in Murder Trials'. *Law Text Culture*, vol. 14, 2010 (https://ro.uow.edu.au/cgi/viewcontent.cgi?article=1257&context=ltc, last accessed October 19, 2021).

Menon, Madhavi. 'The Presumption of the Penis'. *The Asian Age*, July 16, 2012 (http://archive.asianage.com/columnists/presumption-penis-527, last accessed October 19, 2021).

Menon, Nivedita. *Recovering Subversion: Feminist Politics Beyond the Law*. 1st ed., Orient Blackswan Private Limited, 2007.

——. *Gender and Politics in India*. Oxford University Press, 1999.

Mitra, Durba. *Indian Sex Life: Sexuality and the Colonial Origins of Modern Social Thought*. Princeton University Press, 2020.

Mody, Perveez. *Intimate State: Love-Marriage and the Law in Delhi*. Routledge India, 2019.

Mody, Zia. *10 Judgements That Changed India*. Penguin, 2013.

Narrain, Arvind. *Queer: 'Despised Sexuality', Law and Social Change*. Books for Change, 2004.

——, and Alok Gupta. *Law like Love: Queer Perspectives on Law*. Yoda Press, 2011.

Nelson, Dean. 'India's first married lesbian couple given 24-hour protection'. *The Telegraph*, July 26, 2011 (https://www.telegraph.co.uk/news/worldnews/asia/india/8662082/Indias-first-married-lesbian-couple-given-24-hour-protection.html, last accessed October 19, 2021).

Nizami Ganjavi. *Layla-Majnun*. Prose adaptation by Colin Turner. John Blake, 1997.

Nussbaum, Martha C. 'India: Implementing Sex Equality Through Law'. *The Gender of Constitutional Jurisprudence*, vol. 2, no. 1, January 4, 2001, pp. 35–58 (https://chicagounbound.uchicago.edu/cjil/vol2/iss1/4).

Oldenburg, Veena Talwar. 'Lifestyle as Resistance: The Case of the Courtesans of Lucknow, India'. *Feminist Studies*, vol. 16, no. 2, 1990, pp. 259–87 (https://doi.org/10.2307/3177850).

Parker, Kunal M. '"A Corporation of Superior Prostitutes": Anglo-Indian Legal Conceptions of Temple Dancing Girls, 1800–1914'. *Modern Asian Studies*, vol. 32, no. 3, July 1998, pp. 559–633 (https://doi.org/10.1017/S0026749X98003187).

Parthasarathy, Suhrith. 'The need for an anti-discrimination law'. *The Hindu*, June 15, 2020 (https://www.thehindu.com/opinion/lead/the-need-for-an-anti-discrimination-law/article31828372.ece, last accessed October 19, 2021).

Rajan, Rajeswari Sunder. 'Women between Community and State: Some implications of the Uniform Civil Code debates in India'. *Social Text*, vol. 18, no. 4, ser. 65, December 1, 2000, pp. 55–82 (https://doi.org/10.1215/01642472-18-4_65-55).

Ravichandran, Nayantara. 'Legal Recognition of Same-Sex Relationships in India'. *Journal of Indian Law and Society*, vol. 5.

Rich, Timothy S. 'Taiwan's Same-Sex Marriage Breakthrough, in Context'. *The Diplomat*, May 26, 2017 (https://thediplomat.com/2017/05/taiwans-same-sex-marriage-breakthrough-in-context/, last accessed October 19, 2021).

Rowen, Beth. 'Important Supreme Court Decisions in Lesbian, Gay, Bisexual, and Transgender History'. *Infoplease*, February 17, 2017 (https://www.infoplease.com/us/government/judicial-branch/important-supreme-court-decisions-in-lesbian-gay-bisexual-and-transgender-history, last accessed October 19, 2021).

Roy, Anupama. *Gendered Citizenship: Historical and Conceptual Explorations*. Orient Blackswan, 2013.

Sahai, Vikramaditya. 'The Sexual Is Political: Consent and the Transgender Persons (Protection of Rights) Act, 2019'. Official website of the Centre for Law and Policy Research, February 3, 2020 (https://clpr.org.in/blog/the-sexual-is-political-consent-and-the-transgender-persons-protection-of-rights-act-2019/, last accessed October 19, 2021).

———. 'CLPR | Transform International Conference Speaker Series: Vikramaditya Sahai'. YouTube, July 10, 2018 (https://www.youtube.com/watch?v=G4TVK2dRp-4, last accessed October 19, 2021).

Salmon, Owen. 'The Crimes Concerning Brothels, Pimps and Prostitution'. In *Law Made Simple: Compliance for Business, Citizens and for our Government* (available online: https://lawfulliving.co.za/book/text/law-enforcement—brothels.html, last accessed October 19, 2021).

Sarkar, Tanika. *Hindu Wife, Hindu Nation: Community, Religion, and Cultural Nationalism*. Indiana University Press, 2010.

Sengar, Shweta. 'LGBT Rights: Students From IITs Are Protesting Section 377 of IPC; file petition in SC'. *IndiaTimes*, May 15, 2018 (https://www.indiatimes.com/news/india/lgbt-rights-students-from-iits-are-protesting-section-377-of-ipc-file-petition-in-sc-345422.html, last accessed October 19, 2021).

Shah, A.B., ed. *The Roots of Obscenity, Obscenity Literature and the Law*. Lalvani Publishing House, 1968.

Shah, Svati B. 'True Sex and the Law: Prostitution, Sodomy, and the Politics of Sexual Minoritization in India'. In Srivastava, *Sexuality Studies*, pp. 161–83.

Sharafi, Mitra June. *Law and Identity in Colonial South Asia: Parsi Legal Culture 1772–1947*. Permanent Black, 2017.

Shinde, Tarabai, and Rosalind O'Hanlon. *A Comparison between Women and Men: Tarabai Shinde and the Critique of Gender Relations in Colonial India*. Oxford University Press, 1994.

Shourie, Arun. *Courts and Their Judgments: Premises, Prerequisites, Consequences*. Rupa, 2002.

Singh, Mahendra Pal, et al. *The Indian Legal System: An Enquiry*. Oxford University Press, 2019.

Singh, Sarva Daman. *Polyandry in Ancient India*. Vikas Publishing House, 1978.

Sinha, Bhadra. 'SC says privacy is fundamental right, ruling may impact Aadhaar, gay sex law'. *Hindustan Times*, August 24, 2017 (https://www.hindustantimes.com/india-news/right-to-privacy-is-a-guaranteed-fundamental-right-says-supreme-court/story-KvePlHt4UZK5igK0ecG6AL.html, last accessed October 19, 2021).

Soneji, Davesh. *Unfinished Gestures: Devdāsīs, Memory, and Modernity in South India*. University of Chicago Press, 2012.

Srinivasan, Rama. *Courting Desire*. Rutgers University Press, 2020.

Srivastava, Sanjay, ed. *Sexuality Studies*. Oxford University Press, 2013.

Stephens, Julia Anne. *Governing Islam: Law, Empire, and Secularism in South Asia*. Cambridge University Press, 2018.

Vanita, Ruth. 'The Special Marriage Act: Not Special Enough'. *Manushi*, no. 58, 1990.

Venkatesan, J. 'Supreme Court sets aside Delhi HC verdict decriminalising gay sex'. *The Hindu*, August 17, 2016 (https://www.thehindu.com/news/national/supreme-court-sets-aside-delhi-hc-verdict-decriminalising-gay-sex/article5446939.ece, last accessed October 19, 2021).

Weitzer, R. 'Legalizing Prostitution: Morality Politics in Western Australia'. *British Journal of Criminology*, vol. 49, no. 1, 2009, pp. 88–105 (https://doi.org/10.1093/bjc/azn027).

ANNEXURE III

Court Cases & Statutes

CRIMINAL

Court Cases

Asokan K.M. vs The Superintendent of Police, WP (Crl) No. 297 of 2016 (S).

Safiya Sultana vs State of UP, Habeas Corpus No. 16907 of 2020.

Shafin Jahan vs Asokan K.M. & Ors, (2018) 16 SCC 368.

Justice K.S. Puttaswamy vs Union of India, WP (Crl) No. 494 of 2012.

Smt. Bimla Devi vs Chaturvedi & Ors, AIR 1953 All 613.

Mohd. Ahmed Khan vs Shah Bano Begum, 1985 AIR 945.

Baby Manji Yamada vs Union of India & Anr, (2008) 13 SCC 518.

Danial Latifi vs Union of India, WP (C) 868 of 1986.

Banumathi vs The Regional Manager, WP (MD) No. 6514 of 2014 & MP (MD) No. 1 of 2014.

Joseph Shine vs Union of India, (2019) 2 SCC (Cri) 84.

Statutes

The Surrogacy (Regulation) Bill, 2016

The Dissolution of Muslim Marriages Act, 1939

The Abducted Persons (Recovery and Restoration) Act, 1949

Muslim Women (Protection of Rights on Divorce) Act, 1986

The Muslim Women (Protection of Rights on Marriage) Bill, 2017

The Muslim Women (Protection of Rights on Marriage) Bill, 2019
The Hindu Marriage Act, 1955
The Special Marriage Act, 1954
The Hindu Succession Act, 1956
Uttar Pradesh Prohibition of Unlawful Religious Conversion Ordinance, 2020

IMMORAL

Court Cases

Indian Hotel and Restaurants... vs The State of Maharashtra Through..., 2006 (3) BomCR 705, WP (C) No. 24 of 2017.
Indian Hotel and Restaurant Association (AHAR) & Anr vs The State of Maharashtra & Ors, 2006 (3) BomCR 705.
National Legal Services Authority vs Union of India, AIR 2014 SC 1863.
Smt. Shama Bai & Anr vs State of Uttar Pradesh, Lucknow, AIR 1959 All 57.
Re: Saride Narayana & Ors vs Unknown on 23 February, 1950, AIR 1950 Mad 615.
Pramod Bhagwan Nayak vs State of Gujarat, (2007) 1 GLR 796.
Gaurav Jain vs Union of India & Ors, 1990 SCC 709.
Re: Devakumar & Ors vs Unknown (1970).
Nimeshbhai Bharatbhai Desai vs State of Gujarat, R/Cr MA/26957/2017.
Devakumar & Ors vs Unknown, (1972) 1 MLJ 200.

Statutes

The Madras Devadasi (Prevention of Dedication) Act, 1947
Convention for Suppression of Traffic in Persons and of the Exploitation of the Prostitution of Others, 1950

Suppression of Immoral Traffic Act, 1956
Immoral Traffic Prevention Act, 1986
Devadasi (Prevention of Dedication) Act, 1988
Andhra Pradesh Devadasi (Prohibition of Dedication) Act, 1988
Trafficking of Persons (Prevention, Protection and Rehabilitation) Bill, 2016

OBSCENE

Court Cases

3 Aces A Partnership Firm vs Commissioner of Police, WP No. 1251 of 1981.
Brother John Antony vs The State, 1992 CriLJ 1352.
Major Singh Lachhman Singh vs The State, AIR 1963 PH 443.
Maqbool Fida Husain vs Raj Kumar Pandey, Crl Rev P 282/07.
Kamlesh Vaswani vs Union of India, WP (C) No. 177/2013.
Shreya Singhal vs Union of India, WP (Crl) No. 167 of 2012.
Vidyadharan vs State of Kerala, Appeal (Crl) 278 of 1997.
Amitabh Bachhan Corporation Ltd vs Om Pal Singh Hoon, 1996 (37) DRJ 352.
Aveek Sarkar & Anr vs State of West Bengal & Anr, on 3 February, 1947, Criminal Appeal No. 902 of 2004.
C.T. Prim & Anr vs The State, AIR 1961 Cal 177.
Chandra Rajakumari & Anr vs Commissioner of Police, 1998 (1) ALD 810.
Cohen vs California, 403 U.S. 15 (1971)
Devidas Ramachandra Tuljapurkar vs State of Maharashtra & Ors, Criminal Appeal No. 1179 of 2010.
Dharmendra Dhirajlal Soneji vs State of Gujarat, (1997) 1 GLR 198.
Jacobellis vs Ohio, 378 U.S. 184 (1964).

K.A. Abbas vs The Union of India & Anr, 1971 AIR 481.

K. Ramakrishnan & Anr vs State of Kerala & Ors, AIR 1999 Ker 385.

Kailash Chandra & Ors vs Emperor, AIR 1932 Cal 651.

Khirode Chunder Roy Chowdhury vs Emperor, 13 Ind Cas 993.

Mr R. Basu vs National Capital Territory of Delhi & Anr, 2007 CriLJ 4254.

Ms A. Arulmozhi vs The Government of India, WP No. 24430 of 2004.

Narendra H. Khurana & Ors vs Commissioner of Police & Anr, 2004 CriLJ 3393.

Neelam Mahajan Singh vs Commissioner of Police, 1996 CriLJ 2725.

Pawan Kumar vs State of Haryana & Anr, 1996 SCC (4) 17.

Pratibha Naitthani vs Union of India (UoI) & Ors, AIR 2006 Bom 259.

Railway Board, Govt Of India vs M/S Observer Publications (P) Ltd, 1972 AIR 1792.

Ramanlal Lalbhai Desai vs Central Board of Film Certification, AIR 1988 Bom 278.

Ranjit D. Udeshi & Ors vs The State, AIR 1962 Bom 268.

Ranjit D. Udeshi vs State of Maharashtra, 1965 AIR 881.

Sadhna vs State, 19 (1981) DLT 210.

Santosh Kumar Gupta vs K.P. Singh Dev & Ors, 1995 (0) MPLJ 944.

State vs Thakur Prasad & Ors, AIR 1959 All 49.

The State vs Dina Nath & Ors, AIR 1956 PH 85.

Union of India (UoI) & Ors vs Film Federation of India & Anr, 1989 (3) BomCR 377.

Zafar Ahmad Khan vs The State, AIR 1963 All 105.

Prithi Chand vs State of Himachal Pradesh, 1989 AIR 702.

Nimeshbhai Bharatbhai Desai vs State of Gujarat, R/Cr MA/26957/2017.

Pramod Bhagwan Nayak vs State of Gujarat, (2007) 1 GLR 796.
Indian Hotel and Restaurant Association (AHAR) & Anr vs The State of Maharashtra & Ors, WP (C) No. 576 of 2016.
Sanjay Kishan Kaul vs Pushpa Sathyanarayna, WP No. 1215 and 20372 of 2015 and Criminal Original Petition No. 7086 and 7153 of 2015.
Fathima A.S. vs State of Kerala, 2020.

Statutes

The Information Technology Rules, 2011
Section 292, Indian Penal Code
Section 294, Indian Penal Code
Section 354A, Indian Penal Code

UNNATURAL

Court Cases

Anusha Kumari vs Rohan, Civil Writ Jurisdiction Case No. 5689 of 2015.
Nimeshbhai Bharatbhai Desai vs State of Gujarat, (2018) SCC 732.
K.M. Nanavati vs State of Maharashtra, 1962 AIR 605.
M. Chinna Karuppasamy vs Kanimozhi, 2015 CriLJ 4523.
Moti @ Mohit vs State (NCT Of Delhi), Criminal Appeal No. 614/2010.
Rajee vs Baburao, AIR 1996 Mad 262.
Subrata Kumar Banerjee vs Dipti Banerjee, AIR 1974 Cal 61.
Suresh Kumar Koushal & Ors vs Naz Foundation (India) Trust & Ors, SLP (Civil) No. 15436 of 2009 & Ors, (2014) 1 SCC 1.
Indian Young Lawyers Association vs State of Kerala, WP (C) No. 373 of 2006 (See https://indiankanoon.org/doc/163639357/, last accessed October 19, 2021).

Kantaru Rajeevaru vs Indian Young Lawyers Association, Review Petition (C) No. 3358/2018 (See https://www.sci.gov.in/pdf/JUD_6.pdf, last accessed October 19, 2021).

Statutes

Report of the Expert Committee on the Issues relating to Transgender Persons, 2014

The Protection of Women from Domestic Violence Act, 2015

Section 377, Indian Penal Code

Section 497, Indian Penal Code

Transgender Persons (Protection of Rights) Act, 2019

Protection of Children from Sexual Offences Act, 2012

Information Technology Act, 2000

Transgender Persons (Protection of Rights) Rules, 2020

Indian Penal Code (Amendment) Bill, 2019

Kerala Hindu Places of Public Worship (Authorisation of Entry) Rules, 1965

Acknowledgments

A non-lawyer writing a book on the law needs to rely on strong legal minds for support. I am very grateful to the legal expertise of Vasuman Khandelwal, Upendra Baxi, Ratna Kapur, Prashanto Sen, Ajay Gandhi, Shyam Gopal, Bharat Jairaj, Chitra Narayan, Ritin Rai, and Kunal M. Parker.

My legal and non-legal desires were supported and encouraged by a wide circle of friends and family. In Delhi, Jonathan Gil Harris (steeped in the sweetness of jaggery), Amma and Achan, Shohini Ghosh, Poonam Saxena, Anupama Chandra, and Mandakini Dubey nourished both the book and its author. In far-flung lands, Lee Edelman, Nandini Gopinadh, Vishnu Balchand, Nikhil and Rohan and Zippy Menon-Schjerning, Kalyani Menon, Kevin Schjerning, Judith Brown, Ashley T. Shelden, Bill Cohen, Freyan Panthaki, and Nayanika Mathur were the icing on the cake.

My students, both in and out of class, my invaluable research assistants, especially Ketan Jain and Diya Mukhedkar, my priceless editors, Ravi Singh and Nazeef Mollah, and my co-conspirator, Shiv Datt Sharma—thanks to you all.

This book is dedicated to my grandfather, N. Gopala Menon, whom I never met, but who injected the legal genes into my family. And to my beloved father, T. Mohan Chander Menon, who encouraged my passion for argumentation, and who, devastatingly, passed away before he could see this iteration of it.